Writing Science Fiction

What If?

Writing Science Fiction

What If?

Lazette Gifford

Aber publishing

© 2010 Lazette Gifford
© 2010 Cover design GLMP Ltd

ISBN: 978-1-84285-060-2

First published by Aber Publishing, PO Box 225, Abergele, LL18 9AY, United Kingdom.

Website: http://www.aber-publishing.co.uk

All rights reserved. No part of this book may be reproduced or stored in an information retrieval system without the express permission of the publishers given in writing.

The moral rights of the author have been asserted.

Typeset by Bookcraft Ltd, Stroud, Gloucestershire.

Printed and bound in Europe.

Contents

	Preface	**1**
1	**Defining Science Fiction**	**7**
	Science and science fiction	7
	Hard science fiction	10
	Soft science fiction	12
	The subgenres	14
	Media-based science fiction	19
	What is speculative fiction?	20
2	**What if Cars Could Fly?**	**21**
	The basics of research	21
	The future is now	23
	Extrapolating small changes into big ones	24
	The science in science fiction	26
	Near-future science fiction	27
3	**Worldbuilding for Terrans**	**29**
	Approaching the art of worldbuilding	29
	Technology of the future	30
	Future weapons and future war	33
	Defining human cultures in other places	34
	Living quarters and entertainment	36
	The tricky question of religion and the future	37
	The future of humanity	40
4	**Building New Worlds**	**45**
	Worldbuilding: the wide view	45
	The stars	46
	The worlds	48
	Understanding biomes	49
	Alien weather	52

5 Extra Arms Do Not Make an Alien — 57

Defining *their* world — 57
Extra arms and wings — 60
Some aliens are more alien than others — 62
One thing leads to another — 63
Technology, form and culture — 67
The daily life of aliens — 69
Naming aliens — 73

6 Language of the Future — 75

Writing for today's reader — 75
Creating future words and slang — 76
Dealing with alien languages — 77
Move beyond the words — 80

7 Staying Close to Home — 83

Placing a story on Earth — 83
The pitfalls of staying too close to Earth — 85
The first colonies — 86
Moving away from Earth — 88

8 Space Travel Possibilities — 93

Home or away — 93
Exploring the galaxy — 94
Drive technologies — 96
Ship types — 99
Sometimes the story is the journey — 103
Who wants an adventure? — 103

9 Who is In Charge Here? — 107

The future rule — 107
United we stand? — 113
Alone or with others — 115
How communications influence government — 116

10 It's All Been Done Before 119

The challenge of writing something new 119
Clichés and mainstays of science fiction 120
Time travel stories 122
Bug-eyed monsters and invasion Earth 124
Relying too much on media science fiction 125

11 Creating the Characters of Tomorrow 127

Which comes first, plot or characters? 127
The four types of characters 128
Creating heroes 129
Creating villains 131
Special problems with protagonists and antagonists 134
Secondary characters 135
Other characters 137
Working with alien characters 138
Using archetypes 140
Soldier, baker, technoplasma light maker 143

12 Pulling it All Together 147

The work of writing the story 147
Developing the background 149
Titles 157
Plotting the future 159
Story creation 160
Working with outlines 163
How to keep stories moving forward 167

13 Working Like a Professional 173

Setting goals and making schedules 173
Writing, rewriting and editing 176
Edit now or later? 178
Getting outside help 180
Two questions to ask about the story 181
Checking the story one last time 182

14. This Little Book Went to Market — 185

Time to move on	185
Checking bookshop shelves	186
Alternative markets	188
Submission packages and query letters	191
Synopsis	196
Looking professional	197
Accepting rejection	198

Epilogue — 201

Reading List for Science Fiction — 203

Selected Bibliography — 209

Index — 211

Preface

Imagining the future

People often ask those of us who create science fiction why we don't write *real* stories instead. It's hard to explain the draw of this genre to someone who can't imagine life outside the norms of here and now. Those of us who write science fiction see things a little differently and look to the possible instead of reality.

Though it may not seem it at first glance, writing science fiction is an inherently optimistic pastime. No matter how dark and dystopian the future (or alternate) world created by the writer, the tale still reflects the fundamental belief that humans, or something like them, survived to be there. We may write tales of global war, alien invasions, or a more subtle fall of civilization, but our stories are almost always about the humans who exist there, surviving against the odds.

Predicting the future is a tricky business. Although some authors spend considerable time trying to keep watch over new discoveries in the sciences or keep tabs on changing trends in society, they are often caught off-guard by something which upsets theories and beliefs that prevailed only a short time before. Sometimes things change so quickly that a story the author wrote last year may be out of date before it sees print. Consider that Pluto is no longer considered a planet, or how finding ice on Mars has changed our knowledge of that world. Both of these recent adjustments dramatically altered our view of the solar system; as a result, science fiction novels set on Mars or Pluto that were published *before* those modifications and discoveries now appear dated.

We create stories based on speculation and imagination. Those who imagine a future in which aliens come to Earth are being no less realistic, in the world of science fiction, than those who predict a universe devoid of all intelligent life outside our world. For the science fiction writer, the future is an empty slate on which anything can be written, even though some of those things may not be probable. The distinctions between possible and probable are often blurred in science fiction novels. If that makes such works seem unreal, remember that a hundred years ago the idea of travelling to the moon or sending a spacecraft to Mars would have been considered impossible by most people. The wavering line between unreal and possible shifts with every new invention and discovery.

Some people enjoy writing science fiction stories that take today's problems and put them into a new setting where the author can explore possible solutions without dealing with the emotional baggage that comes from a tale set in the present day. Taking a current day situation and extrapolating the same basic situation into a story based a thousand years from now can also deliver a tale that resonates with readers, drawing them into a new world that has obvious parallels with their own.

Science of all sorts is the basis from which a science fiction story grows. Both hard and soft sciences can create exceptional stories. The choice of what to base a new future on depends on the writer and what sort of tale the writer wants to tell. There is no science fiction that is inherently better or worse than another type. If the reader enjoys the story, then it has succeeded in what it was meant to do.

In *Twenty Thousand Leagues Under the Sea*, one of the earliest examples of science fiction, Jules Verne's famous Nautilus was based on Robert Fulton's steam-engine driven submarine. Building on what is already invented and expanding it into a viable story has always been the mainstay of science fiction. But how does a person learn how to make those leaps of imagination? They do so by looking around them at the world today.

We are living in a science fiction world.

Between 1900 and 1950, society changed irrevocably. In 1900 horses were still the primary mode of transportation but by 1950 in all but the poorest countries they had been sent to pasture to become expensive pets, replaced by cars and other vehicles for farming and transportation. The art of war changed for ever during this period as well. During World War I, horse cavalry went up against huge metal suits of armour on wheels – the first primitive tanks. But by the end of World War II, using horses in battle was over; the unfortunate demise of the Polish Cavalry during the early years of that war signalled that change. Another change was atomic power: for good or bad, it was let loose from Pandora's Box. Telephones, already present by 1900, spread throughout the world and television steadily spread to replace the then still-new radio as the standard of entertainment and news gathering in many homes by mid-century. All of these changes marked a huge difference in the way of life for people in countries experiencing the expansion of scientific theory into reality during the early twentieth century.

In the second half of the twentieth century the changes we face may not seem so great at first glance, but they have had as far-reaching effects on our lives. The ancient tale of Icarus falling when his wings melted has given way to the reality of thousands of jet-lagged commuters, with travellers hopping daily from one continent to another. But changes that are meant to help improve our lives often generate problems of their own. For instance, pesticides created to help farmers have proven in some cases to be a hidden menace. So not all changes are obviously for the better, and some of the best changes still come with a dark side. We live our lives in the balance, hoping that what we have developed will prove more good than bad. This is an important aspect of life to recall when creating a future. In a tale where the balance has slipped, it might not be because something was purposely pushed over the edge.

There are, however, some very important innovations in the world that we already take for granted, such as video recording devices, microwave ovens, digital cameras and home computers. Communications has been completely changed by our digital age, both through the Internet and by cell phones. The communicators of the original *Star Trek* series look bulky compared to the cell phones of today. Go grab your DVD copy of the original *Star Trek* series and take a look at them. Drop some popcorn in the microwave, and sit back for an hour of enjoyment – entertainment you can have at any time you want, rather than tied to some set hours. Watch the show again and again. Go to the Internet and chat with someone half a world away and share your feelings about the show. These are some of the changes we already take for granted.

So the world has changed. We are no longer limited to our neighbourhoods for companionship or survival. These are huge changes, though most people don't realize it because they've grown used to them. However, some writers of the past had envisioned snippets of this future, even if written in their own odd ways. Computers have always been a part of the science fiction landscape. How often did characters in those books grab food from some electronic box, already cooked and ready to eat? Yes, we're still looking for our aircars and personal jet packs, but reading Dick Tracy comics and the 'Wow-look-at-that!' wristwatch communicator of yesterday appears quaint and cute by today's technological standards.

Arthur C. Clarke imagined communications satellites in orbit around the Earth; today we are living with the reality. You may not imagine something that becomes reality but you can look at what we have today, including new discoveries in science, and *imagine* where those changes will lead.

There is a finer line between science fiction and fantasy than you might realize and it is far from being a solid wall that separates the two. They blend now and then, and people will often argue about some story aspects like psychic powers or faster-than-light spaceship drives. Some people will consider them to be possibilities not yet explained by science, and others will consider them impossibilities if supposedly based on science as we know it. The tale of a near-future nuclear disaster might end up on the shelves as a thriller rather than the post-apocalyptic tale you thought you were telling. There is no absolute line. People will continue arguing over whether Ann McCaffrey's *Dragons of Pern* is fantasy or science fiction for as long as people read the book.

Here's the bottom line: it doesn't matter. Readers will find the book if that's what they want to read. As a writer, you have to be concerned with the tale you want to tell, and not the tags under which it will be filed. The story must always come first.

Science fiction, in whatever flavour you choose, is the genre of change. The author isn't going to write about the everyday life of a bored housewife or the soul-deadening factory job her husband holds – though those two characters could still exist in a future world. As an author, you are going to look at what the world is like today, study the people around you, and imagine it all transported to a different time or place. If that housewife and husband exist, how are they – and their world – different from the world of today? There must be some difference for it to be science fiction.

When you write a science fiction novel, you are creating a future. It may not be *the* future, though you might be one of the few who chance upon some link between now and another time and, like Verne and Clarke, have your name associated as much with reality as with the imagination. Even if you miss the link to something tangible, you might still create stories people read with enthusiasm and talk about for years to come. Science fiction, like all fiction, is primarily meant to entertain. It does not have to predict the future or teach the reader – though some stories might do both.

In many ways, we cannot define and limit science fiction. In that respect, this book is only to whet your imagination and help you consider various aspects of creation that will help you visualize and create your own unique world. What you imagine is part of who you are, and what you see, feel and imagine will be important in your future. You are a visionary.

So the next time someone asks you why you write these stories, and not something *real* instead, tell him it's because you are not tied to one place and time, and what you write about is no different, in essence, from the author who writes about a plane crash or how a gang war gets out of hand in a big city. None of it is real; all of it is based on what the author sees as possibilities based on the world of today. Science fiction writers just have a wider view.

1 Defining Science Fiction

It's not all aliens and fast ships

- Science and science fiction
- Hard science fiction
- Soft science fiction
- The subgenres
- Media-based science fiction
- What is speculative fiction?

In this chapter we'll look at the basis on which science fiction stories are defined and explore some of the more popular types. This is a brief overview and cannot begin to explore the genre in any depth. Rather, these descriptions are intended to help you understand that there are many facets of the science fiction world and that you need not be limited in what lines you want to pursue. Deciding which flavours of science fiction appeal to you is the first step in creating the story you want to tell.

Science and science fiction

Two terms are often associated with science fiction: the 'wow factor' and the 'sense of wonder.' Both of these relate to how the stories affect the readers and they are as essential to a science fiction story as any science you bring to the tale. In many ways, the science is the easier part since it can be researched. The 'sense of wonder' is the soul of the story, while the science is the brain. Both are essential to telling a compelling science fiction tale.

Science theory does not create science fiction stories; it is only the window through which the writer sometimes views a new world. For example, understanding how quantum physics can explain the behaviour of very small particles may give you an idea for a good story, but having this knowledge is not necessary to create a tale that will intrigue readers. Understanding how science affects people is more important, in many cases, than understanding how the science itself works. You do not need to know how a microwave oven works to know how it has changed our world.

Physics, astrophysics, and nanotechnology are not the only sciences of the future; biology, botany and cultural anthropology are all equally viable sciences to use when looking at the future. Most people will say that the stories based in the mathematical sciences are 'hard science fiction' while those based in the others are 'soft science fiction.' Others will define hard science fiction as those fictional works based on scientific theory, and soft science fiction as those based on human experience.

The terms hard and soft are not a reflection on how well the book is written, or how strong the story is – they are only designations between one type of science fiction and another. You'll see plenty of other tags as well: space opera, cyberpunk, post-apocalyptic and many others. As people, we are always trying to pigeon-hole things into their proper slot but, as with most of real life, science fiction stories are not always easy to categorize. New terms will come into being and old ones will become slighted as *old-fashioned* even when they are used to describe tales of the far future on wondrous, exciting worlds. Then, a few years later, such stories will come back into vogue again when someone writes such a story and people connect with it again.

Anyone who reads a lot of science fiction (and anyone who is trying to write science fiction should fit this category) knows that genres leap up in popularity all the time and then die down again as something else takes their place. If you are writing something but you don't see many similar works on the shelves, don't worry. Chances are it will become popular again because there is always a steady readership for various types of science fiction.

Movie and television shows can influence what is prevalent on the shelves. If a popular science fiction movie has a cyberpunk theme, then the cyberpunk book market will bloom again. You might even take note of upcoming movies

Defining Science Fiction

and, if you happen to have something already written, time your submission with the opening of a similar movie. It is far harder to write something after the movie has become popular, though, because by the time you get the work done and submitted, it's likely that the market will be over-saturated with stories of that type. It's not a good idea to write something solely to try to play to that type of market – though if you have an idea you really want to try, there's no reason not to. It just may take longer to sell than expected.

Another division between hard and soft science fiction falls in the category of what is possible given our current knowledge of science, and what isn't. Many hard science fiction aficionados will not admit either faster-than-light space travel or time travel stories into the hard science fiction category. Others consider *The Time Machine* by H.G. Wells as one of the quintessential science fiction stories.

In other words, not only the terms used but also what is considered science fiction has always been fluid, and worrying too much about whether your manuscript falls into one category or another shouldn't matter as long as you write the story you want to tell. As an example, while studying various books of both hard and soft science fiction types I repeatedly found books that appeared on both lists, including Isaac Asimov's famous *Foundation* series.

Science fiction should never be tied to rules that might stifle the reach of the imagination or try to limit it to certain views. Science fiction needs the freedom to explore all possibilities, without worrying about what tags will be attached to it.

What if...

Science fiction is a continual game of 'what if...' as the writer looks at how pieces in our world fit together and how changes, both small and great, would change the world. In the exercises sprinkled throughout this book, I'll ask occasional 'what if' questions to help you explore possible science fiction ideas. Please take the time to read through them and consider the possibilities that each 'what if' situation presents. Writing science fiction

> isn't only about the big ideas, but also about how change affects every aspect of life.
>
> For this first exercise, think about how the world has changed in your lifetime. What are the three biggest changes in terms of science, and how did those changes affect the world? What if one or more of them hadn't happened? What would the world be like without one of those inventions that we already take for granted? As an example (given for this first exercise only) consider the microwave oven that I mentioned earlier. Microwave cooking has transformed the time it takes to make some meals. While not all cooking is done in a microwave, it is significant to realize that many restaurants use them to heat sauces or thaw meats, which means less waste from unused foods that were already thawed but not used. So what would have happened if the power of the microwave (located in the 300MHz to 300GHz range) had not been harnessed? Microwaves are used for more than cooking. The microwave bandwidth is used extensively in communications systems, including wireless access to the Internet. It is also used in radio astronomy for remote sensing in air traffic control.

Hard science fiction

In stories that are considered hard science fiction, sciences such as physics, robotics, nanotechnology and astronomy form the basis of the entire story. The mathematical sciences are given top billing in the hard science fiction books; these are tales in which theory and knowledge become real.

Larry Niven based his famous *Ringworld* series on physics, starting with an artificially created world shaped in the form of a gigantic ring, he then peopled the story with a set of interesting explorers. For hard science fiction, though, the logistics of the science have to be sound and *Ringworld* shows not only Niven's education in mathematics but also his understanding of geology, climatology and all the other aspects that make up a working world.

However, if that scientific understanding had been the extent of the work, it would have been an essay, not a story. Niven also has a gift for creating the other two important aspects of a story: characters and plot. He created four characters – two human and two alien – and set them exploring this ringworld oddity to try to learn who had built it. Their adventures made Larry Niven famous both for his excellent use of science and also for a fantastic story.

Theory alone does not make a story. Inspired by the non-fiction essay *Time and Tide* by Isaac Asimov, Niven wrote his Hugo award winning *Neutron Star*. Asimov, himself one of the most famous hard science fiction writers, had seen the theory and science element – but not the story to go with it.

Writing hard science fiction requires research of the type a graduate student might make. If you are going to write about a certain type of real-world science, then you have to immerse yourself in the basics. Unless you are actively working in the field, chances are you need a refresher in some of the material even if you took classes in college. This is not the type of material you can be lax about because the audience for these stories is extremely demanding of authenticity. The science has to be sound and you may have your ideas vetted by those who work in the field – though don't be discouraged if the scientist doesn't see the point in writing a fiction story.

No matter what type of science fiction you write, the science must be integral to the plot, rather than something added on and which hasn't any real function in the story. So, while having a scientific background can be a real boon to writing stories based on hard science, that doesn't mean a layperson cannot attempt these types of tales. It does mean, however, that such a person will have considerable work researching the background. A good place to start is with current scientific magazines such as *New Scientist, Scientific American* and *Popular Science*. If you cannot take out a subscription, try your local library for reference copies and plan to spend a few hours each week looking through the material.

If you haven't already decided on a specific type of science or theory on which to base your story, take notes on everything that interests you. Once you have settled on the basis of your work, expand your research on the subject and those closely related to it. Read everything you can, but at the same time don't forget that you are writing fiction. Imagine the science in a real-world setting.

The science fiction author must have the ability to work scientific theory into prose in a way which will intrigue and entertain the reader. If you want to tell a story about some scientific discovery or theory, you have to wrap it around realistic characters who fit into their world, and braid the whole into a tale which makes the science as essential and fascinating as the rest of the plot.

> **What if...**
>
> Once again, we're going to look at changes that would affect the world as we know it. For this exercise, consider any technological or scientific aspect of the real world and think about how it might be changed (rather than removed, as in the last exercise) to make a difference in the way we live.

Soft science fiction

In soft science fiction, the understanding of how humans interact is often the core of the story, rather than the science of how they got to where they are. These tales are more concerned with the impact of technology, for instance, than why the science underlying that technology works. The stories often revolve around such sciences as anthropology, philosophy, psychology and sociology rather than the sciences involved in number manipulations.

Dune by Frank Herbert is considered one of the best works in the soft science fiction field. His depiction of a future world often crosses over into the mystical: the mythical power of the House Atreides, and the battles of the various Houses for power, creates a book with a medieval feel set in a far future. But *Dune* is not a world haphazardly thrown together, a thin veneer of another world created to present a tale of power and treachery. Herbert carefully crafted his world of *Dune*, sometimes using an Egyptian base to create a realistic setting.

So soft science fiction is concerned with the human condition and how we react to changes in an imagined future, but the science of how we got to that future is not as fully explained as it would be in hard science fiction. It might disregard some of the rules hard science fiction writers and readers consider essential, including features that would be rejected by hard science fiction purists. For instance, faster-than-light spaceship drives often appear in soft science fiction, as do psychic abilities, multitudes of aliens and time travel.

Choosing to write soft science fiction does not mean you're free to throw anything together as a story background. If you want to write about social upheaval on a newly settled world, then you cannot simply make it Earth with a new name. Your setting must be plausible, including how your people arrived on this world and what drove them to their current problems.

So how do you make a story plausible when you are writing what is considered impossible in today's world? You do so by making something considered improbable a consistent presence within your imagined world, so that it interacts with the rest of what is happening. Consider the difference between these two lines:

A car was hit by a meteorite today.
A fourth car was hit by a meteorite today.

The first line indicates an event, something odd and unusual, and out of the ordinary. The second line shows something already part of history – it has happened before, so it's not such a shock that it happened again. It may be intriguing to the reader, but he will accept it as already integrated into the world. So unless your story is specifically about a change happening right in the story, make certain your additions are already fully incorporated into the world. For example, if you are going to write a tale about time travel, then the repercussions of this ability to travel through time must be present in some way. Have the people of your society learned that the past cannot be changed? Or have they learned their very existence is in flux because of the ability to change history? Every aspect of your story must have a relationship to the other parts. So the science in a hard science fiction story cannot be a thin veneer. Similarly, you also cannot throw improbable science into the mix without testing how it affects the world around the characters.

This part is sometimes especially difficult for people writing a story in which the science fiction is used only as a setting, while another genre is the prime focus. Writing a science fiction mystery or a science fiction romance can lead to sloppy background work when the writer doesn't focus as much on the science fiction elements as on the others. This can easily ruin an otherwise exciting and wonderful story.

> **What if...**
>
> This time, take a look at the society around you and consider 'what ifs' in the form of changes which would have dramatically altered the world if they had never existed. As an example, what if large cities had never existed? If the viable maximum cut-off point for a city's growth had been about 20,000 people, how would it affect how you live? What has this got to do with science fiction?
>
> Consider two different scenarios: A post-apocalyptic Earth where supplying the inhabitants of large cities would be impossible, and the settling of new worlds where it would take generations to get a large enough population to make huge cities.

The subgenres

The subgenres of science fiction are fluid and ever-changing. Science fiction is always in the midst of the 'next big thing' (which might actually be a recycling of an older theme). Space opera comes and goes, and comes back again. Cyberpunk was once such a 'new' thing, but is now relegated to the normal and expected.

You cannot predict what will become important in the field of science fiction. You cannot rely on writing for the 'next big thing' either. If suddenly books about life on asteroids become popular, by the time you write, edit and submit a novel with this type of story, chances are the market will already have moved on. And worse, the publisher will have looked at dozens of these books already and will not be very interested in seeing the same old story again.

Short story writers have a slightly better chance of cashing in on a new trend, but there will be hundreds of other writers with the same plan to write for the new trend. Writing to the market is a tricky business. Generally, you will do much better to write the story you want to tell, without regard to what others are doing. The only time this isn't true is when you are writing for a very specific market, which might be a magazine with a limited range of interests, or an anthology with a specific theme.

Knowing some of the subgenres can be inspirational, however. Here are a few. Like everything in science fiction, they are apt to grow and change with little warning.

Cyberpunk

Cyberpunk deals with worlds in which technology, usually in the form of government or corporate computers and associated culture, has a stranglehold on life. The main character is usually a loner, tech-savvy and ready to take on the work of bringing down the powers that be. Cyberpunk tends to be dystopian in vision and usually is set in the near future. *Neuromancer* by William Gibson is the definitive novel of this subgenre and many of Philip K. Dick's novels also fall into the category.

Dystopian

The future is not always bright and filled with hope in science fiction. Dystopian books deal with oppressive social control and attempts to direct mankind to a certain way of life. Sometimes the social settings are utopias that have taken a wrong turn, other times they are dictatorships from the very start.

Some of the books in this category are George Orwell's *Nineteen Eighty-Four* and Aldous Huxley's *Brave New World*, as well as *Stand on Zanzibar* by John Brunner, *The Handmaid's Tale* by Margaret Atwood and *Fahrenheit 451* by Ray Bradbury.

It seems as though utopias are few in the science fiction world, and those we do find usually only appear to be perfect but are hiding some dark underside. But works involving dystopian futures abound in science fiction, and remain quite popular.

Alternate history (including steampunk)

Alternate history books are the ultimate 'what if' stories. What if Caesar hadn't been killed? What if Hitler had won? What if the colonies in America had lost their war of independence against Britain? Alternate history novels look at what possibilities could arise if history had been different, exploring what future worlds might look like. Some books in this genre are *Guns of the South* by Harry Turtledove, *Fatherland* by Robert Harris and *The Man in the High Castle* by Philip K. Dick.

Steampunk is most often set in a Victorian world in which steam-powered equipment developed along the same lines as our petrol-driven engines. Quite often the feel of the story is much like cyberpunk, with the disillusioned hero fighting against the government or corporate powers. The classic work of this type is *The Time Machine* by H.G. Wells, more recently *The Difference Engine* by William Gibson and Bruce Sterling is another excellent example.

Space opera

Space opera is one of the mainstays of science fiction, though it occasional falls out of favour. Readers of science fiction often come to it for the pure adventure of travelling to far-flung worlds, fighting battles against menacing aliens, and surviving against the odds. Space opera is the heart of science fiction.

Some of the classics in science fiction fall into the space opera category, including much of the writing by Robert Heinlein and Andre Norton. Many space opera books come in series, such as the *Foreigner Sequence* and the *Chanur Books* by C. J. Cherryh, the *Lensmen* series by E. E. Smith, the *Uplift* books by David Brin and the *Known Space* stories by Larry Niven.

Sociological science fiction

While hard science fiction focuses on the technical side of science fiction, soft science fiction does the same with the human aspects of life. Sociological science fiction examines transformations in society and how they change the future. These transformations can be rooted in scientific discoveries, such as in Nancy Kress's *Beggars in Spain*.

The Left Hand of Darkness by Ursula K. Le Guin is a classic in the realm of sociological science fiction. So is *Dhalgren* by Samuel R. Delany, though it might also fall into the post-apocalyptic category as well. In fact, many of the books in the subgenres can often be dropped into more than one category.

Post-apocalyptic science fiction

Post-apocalyptic stories come in many varieties, from the survival of a handful of people after a nuclear war, to devastation caused by natural disasters, to world-wide destruction by alien invaders.

These are stories of courage and ingenuity in the face of disaster and they sometimes bridge the gap between science fiction and mainstream literature for people who are not otherwise interested in science fiction books.

Lucifer's Hammer by Larry Niven and Jerry Pournelle is a fascinating look at life after a meteorite strike. Nevil Shute's famous *On the Beach* is set after a nuclear war. And sometimes subgenres co-exist: post-apocalyptic stories can be straight adventure stories, but the framework allows writers to comment on current society as seen in sociological science fiction. Heinlein's *Farnham's Freehold* is a noted example of this. Likewise, the glut of 'alien invasion' stories in the classic era of the 1950s also allowed writers to tell an allegory tale of people in fear of the end of the world due to then-current Cold War political tensions – or perhaps fear of not-so-alien Communist invaders infiltrating their own society.

Military science fiction

The world of the military, but transported hundreds of years into the future, has created some popular and exciting tales. One of the classics of military science fiction is *Tactics of Mistake* by Gordon R. Dickson, along with the rest of his *Dorsai* series. Robert Heinlein's *Starship Troopers* is another.

This subgenre exploded in popularity from the 1990s onwards, with the advent of *Hammer's Slammers* by David Drake and subsequent stories by this talented author. More recent books include the *Honor Harrington* series by David Weber, the *Serrano Legacy* books by Elizabeth Moon, and

Lois McMaster Bujold's *Vorkosigan Saga*. John Ringo has joined the force with his tales of military SF, but he has also worked to cross over into a variety of subgenres with some stories featuring dragons, as well as stories of pre-industrial worlds.

Space fantasy

Some science fiction books brush along the edge of fantasy; an early example is *The People* stories by Zenna Henderson. Likewise, the *Liaden Universe* books by Steve Miller and Sharon Lee show science fiction blending over into realms sometimes seen in fantasy, as magic and magic-like powers weave through these stories.

Young adult science fiction

The young adult subgenre, also known as juvenile fiction, has a wide appeal to readers of all ages. Like most young adult books of all genres, young adult science fiction usually has a main character in their teens and often deals with their coming of age story. It tends toward adventure stories, from the classic *Tunnel in the Sky* by Robert Heinlein and *Postmarked the Stars* by Andre Norton to *Ender's Game* by Orson Scott Card.

One important point to remember when writing young adult science fiction is not to talk down to the audience or skimp on proper research – neither will win you the respect of the readers. Young adult science fiction may be the first science fiction stories many readers experience and they should be as complex and skilfully written as those in any of the other subgenres.

> ### What if...
>
> Since science fiction is such a large genre, encompassing so many different types of stories, the subgenres are an important and helpful tool for readers to easily connect with the types of stories they like.
>
> For this exercise, find one or two of your favourite science fiction novels (preferably ones that have not been mentioned in this chapter) and decide what subgenre, or

> multiple subgenres, they represent. Some books are easy to classify and some are mavericks that appear to step outside the bounds of classification. However, if you find that many of your own favorites fall into a specific type of subgenre, that is likely to be the type of book you will want to write.

Media-based science fiction

Of all the genres, the media have probably had more impact – both good and bad – on science fiction than on any other type of book. Television, movies and computer games have all influenced how the general public perceives science fiction. Many readers come to the genre through such mega-hits as *Star Wars* and *Star Trek* and are often surprised to find the wider variety of stories science fiction actually encompasses.

Many new writers want to write a book in the *Star Wars*, *Star Trek* or similar universe. But such media-based fiction writing is surrounded by pitfalls, not least of which is that the owner of the original copyright has full control over which books are published for the series. In most cases, they contract someone to write the books and outsiders are rarely accepted into the fold. Some computer game companies run 'open calls' now and then, but generally the writing for an already established universe is done on an invitation-only basis. The copyright owner, typically a company, maintains strict control over what can and cannot be written in such books and the writer is given a set of rules which cannot be broken.

If you want to write for this genre, always approach the work like a professional. Some have found that publishing outside media-based work has helped open the door to contracts, so it is advisable to try your hand at writing original fiction and establishing a name first. Also, keep an eye on official websites and subscribe to the newsletters of any company publishing books for the universe you are interested in. Although it is rare, you might happen upon an open call to submit manuscripts – and if you already write like a professional you will be ahead of 99 per cent of the people who submit.

What is speculative fiction?

The term speculative fiction has been around for some time and can confuse both readers and writers. There is no set definition but, in general, speculative fiction is a catchall phrase for several related genres which usually include science fiction, fantasy and horror. Since these books are often shelved together in stores and libraries, the term has evolved to encompass and explain this link between the three.

Some people consider speculative fiction to be a more literate type of science fiction, with a focus on the language rather than the story. Today the terms are fluid, however, and sometimes it is important to ask what the other person means when using such labels, especially when dealing with publishers.

What if...

For the first time, let's really look at the type of story you'd like to write. Is it hard or soft science fiction? Does it fall into one of the subgenres already mentioned? Don't worry if it doesn't – I've hardly touched on the variations of science fiction filling the shelves of stores and libraries. What if you wanted to start a story right now? What genre and subgenre would it be?

In this chapter, we've glanced over some of the different flavours of science fiction and the subgenres and explored some of the unique possibilities offered in the vast and ever-changing market for these stories.

In the next chapter, we'll start looking at the more concrete aspects of science fiction and how to fill your manuscript with both technology and cultural changes.

2 | What if Cars Could Fly?

- The basics of research
- The future is now
- Extrapolating small changes into big ones
- The science in science fiction
- Near-future science fiction

In this chapter we're going to look at some of the very basic steps in creating a new science fiction world. Worldbuilding – the creation of your entire, integrated future – is the most important aspect of writing science fiction. One way to imagining the future is by looking at what we have now and thinking how it can be changed and adapted to create a new vision of our world. All our current technology is based on the building blocks of earlier technology, and we can trace a line of history from the first shaped-stone tools used to dig furrows in the ground all the way to the huge tractor combines farmers use today. Build your future on today's knowledge, inventions and experiments. Adding new factors into the mix and changing some basics of what we have now can provide a rich and varied new world for your characters.

The basics of research

If you are the type of writer who starts with a character or an incident instead of creating the world first, don't worry. However, early in the story discovery process, you will have to start defining the science fiction aspects of the world in which this person lives and these incidents take place. The order that I take in this book may not be the natural creative order that comes to you as a writer. When you are actually working on a story, the order in which you create your background and characters doesn't matter, but each will impact the other as you will see as we develop the story.

There is hardly a book written, science fiction or not, which hasn't benefited from some research. Science fiction, however, is one of the high-end research genres, along with historical fiction, and a lot of research will be needed. Don't let that idea frighten you away from writing such a story, though. Approaching what you need with a willingness to learn can only benefit your story.

First a few words, though, about organization. If you don't regularly carry a laptop computer with you, then you will need a way to keep notes and easily access them later. It doesn't do you any good to read books and articles, perhaps scribbling a few things on the back of an envelope, if you can't find the information later when you need it. A PDA can be helpful since you can transfer your notes straight to your computer afterwards and easily organize them. However, if you do not have such a device, a small paper notebook will work as well. Small is better than a larger one because it fits into your pocket or purse and you can grab it with ease. This makes it good not only for research notes but for general idea notes as well. If the notebook is large, chances are you won't want to carry it with you all the time.

Notecards are also handy and are easy to sort later. Putting a tag at the top of the card to indicate if it is world-building, character creation, story idea, and so on, will help you later.

Do not be lax in your research and if you use the Internet make certain you double check your information. Wikipedia is very popular, but always remember it is written by people who sometimes don't know as much as they think they do. While many of the errors are caught and corrected, it would be wise to recheck those 'facts.'

Take copious notes – and keep them organized. Take notes on everything you find interesting, whether it fits your current story or not. The more you learn, the more you will have to draw on later to fill out your worlds (and if you make note of the information now, you won't have to go look it up again later for a different manuscript). It can be very frustrating to recall something interesting, but not know when or where you learned it.

So, whenever you come across something make note of it, whether you are actively researching or not. Keeping notes for future work is a great way to generate ideas.

> **What if...**
>
> What if you wanted to write a post-apocalyptic story based on Earth? What subjects would you need to research to find out how your people survive in a world where society has broken down? Make a list of five things you feel would be essential for people to know (note that these items may also be important for stories about colonies set on other worlds, as well). Once you have the list, turn to research and see what basics you can find out about each item. Be certain to write them down in some way and keep them on file. You never know when you might need these things for another story!

The future is now

As I said in the preface, we're living in a science fiction world. Barely a hundred years ago, horse travel was still common in large cities. Looking at how changes in transportation have altered our world can give you a real-world idea of how science fiction works. Did someone, looking at the first cars on the roads of large cities, have an inkling of how much change those cars represented? Imagining those changes is what makes science fiction in its most basic form. There are some stories set far beyond Earth that leave the existence of humans behind, but science fiction is mostly about who we are and what we will do in the future.

With the present energy crisis, we are again standing on the verge of another possible change in transportation and one which might reshape how we travel, including how often and how far we go. This, in turn, could affect the degree of spread and mingling of cultures from around the world as travel has always been a key component to how much we understand others. In previous times, most cross-cultural pollination happened at the borders and crossroads of civilizations. With the advent of nearly instant international communications, we have escaped those borders.

Can we, looking at some small change in our world today, have any idea of how it is going to affect the future? There are several places to look for those changes: transportation, medicine, communications, government, construction and lifestyles. Any of these subjects (and dozens more that you might imagine) can be a starting point for creating a theme for a new science fiction world.

If you are writing science fiction, you want to emphasize how this new world is different from the one in which we live. There can be subtle changes or larger changes, but if it is our world with only a veneer of odd names and gadgets thrown in, then science fiction readers (including publishers) are not going to be interested enough to read the book. Science fiction is about how change affects people and the change has to be as real as the characters you write about.

The world around a person will always have an influence on his actions. A hundred years ago, a man robbing a jewellery store might have expected to get away if he could run fast enough to get clear of the scene. Today, video cameras, police cars and helicopters will make his getaway far more difficult. But what other changes are consequences of these same surveillance devices? Will your character appreciate the safety, or chafe at the lack of privacy that they bring?

Extrapolating small changes into big ones

Everything has an influence on everything else, so when you start looking for something to change for your future world you cannot focus too closely on your change and ignore its wider repercussions. It is doubtful that, when people first ventured into using the Internet and email, many of them thought it would be the virtual downfall of the handwritten letter. And if they did consider it, did they think beyond to the problems it would cause for the postal services? With the lessening of stamped mail, rates rose on everything else they carried. In many countries, this rise in postage costs is causing dire problems for small publishers and magazines. Email may well be the single most important change in our daily lives but it has also affected the phone companies, and it has changed the way many places do business.

Little changes can have huge effects. We all tend to look at the normal things we expect to see change, like our dependence on fossil fuels. But what if (those magic words again) you looked for something more mundane or unusual? Looking beyond the way email has affected the world, let's think about what would happen if someone invented something that truly made paper obsolete. What happens to books? What happens to the stuff already in print? How do businesses use it? How safe is it for secret documents? Perhaps there would be a group of people who memorize things considered too important and secret to be written down. How are they chosen? How are they controlled? If something is created to replace paper itself, and not just something to be used instead of paper for writing purposes, what else can it be used for? If we consider paper as a plant product, could this item also be used to create wood for building?

What if a disease killed all the cattle in the world? Think beyond the loss of a major source of meat and protein. There are also leather goods, for instance. Would cattle ranchers turn to sheep? Sheep need different care. One of the major battles over land in the Wild West occurred when sheep farmers tried to fence off land for their animals in areas where cattle had grazed free in previous times.

So little changes create ripples which spread out and affect other things, setting off new ripples. So you should consider as many implications of your science fiction changes as you can. The future is not merely a new coat of paint on the present; to avoid that impression in your writing, you must examine the depth of the changes you put in place.

> **What if...**
>
> Choose one thing that is commonplace in your everyday life and imagine a world where the item suddenly disappeared. List five things that would be changed because of the disappearance.

The science in science fiction

You do not have to be a rocket scientist to write about space travel. However, you do need to know enough about the basics of space as well as understand how your ship works. The ship may work on something based soundly in scientific fact or it may be something working by extrapolation and imagination – but either way, if your story is about how the ship gets from one place to another, the author needs to have a good, solid understanding of how it does this. Remember, nothing rips the fabric of willing belief in your science fiction story faster than violating the science!

There are other sciences to consider as well, though. Take the idea of a settlement on another world and their worry about atmospheric conditions. Understanding how weather systems work on Earth will give you the basics you need to know about how to manipulate the weather settings for your new world. Studying some of the various cultural groups on Earth – and gaining an understanding of how they adapt to change – can help you create a unique settlement on your new world, rather than a carbon copy of home.

The science in your story can be obvious or subtle; most often it should be multi-layered, weaving various disciplines into new visions of the future. It can be real science blended with supposition and imagination, but the more 'real' you can put into the story, the better it will be. This means you will probably have to study a few things for your books to make certain you have the basics right. For instance, a story where terrorists destroy the water system of your domed colony sounds reasonably straightforward, but it would help if you studied how current systems work, what people have envisioned for better systems, and what people without such systems would have to do to survive this kind of problem.

You will always know more than what you put in your book. You're not going to write a book about the water systems, after all. We generally write stories involving things which already interest us, so the study of these sciences can be as pleasurable as writing about them. As writers of any sort of literature, we should never fear knowledge. You do not have to take a course in water reclamation systems to learn the basics of how they work, or a class in cultural anthropology to be able to read and understand the differences in various cultures spread throughout the world. But everything you learn, whether you use it now or not, becomes fodder for other stories.

Knowledge is a wonderful, recyclable resource as it adds depth to stories and inspires new angles for plots. Knowledge is easy to come by either by spending a few hours in the library or by buying a few books to keep on hand. Used textbooks are especially helpful for some of the sciences as are encyclopedias and scientific periodicals. Study anything that interests you, because what interests you will be what you enjoy writing about as well.

Near-future science fiction

Some stories take place in the near future – in a world we can clearly recognize as our own – and can still be classified as science fiction by the addition of a science fiction mainstay such as an alien invasion, or by something more subtle like an invention which so drastically changes the way of life it would clearly take the world into the realm of science fiction.

The 'fall of civilization' can be the basis for a near-future science fiction story, in which the world of today is changed by a disaster. In such a story, the science research involved would be to understand the nature of the disaster and to study such things as survival techniques and post-disaster psychology.

Near-future science fiction requires meticulous details based in reality. Unlike creating a future where characters either have left Earth or are on an Earth changed by time, the author must make certain the setting corresponds with the world in which he lives.

There is, of course, the problem of drastic changes taking place in the real world which a person cannot foresee. No one imagined New York without the World Trade Center towers or a solar system where Pluto was no longer considered a planet. Stories set too close to our time run the risk of having something drastic change in the real world which makes the fictional near-future story seem 'less real' because the story had not foreseen that change.

This problem can't be helped and it is no reason to avoid writing such a book if you have a story to tell, but it is something to keep in mind as you begin to lay out the basics of your work. Writing science fiction of any type is a risk – after all, the aliens could arrive tomorrow and change everything!

What if...

What change would you expect to see if aliens did arrive tomorrow? What if they came to stay? What if they came only as visitors exploring the galaxy? What would you expect from the aliens and how would knowing that they exist change humanity?

In this chapter we have looked at the basics of research and considered how we already live in a world full of science fiction ideas. We examined the idea of extrapolating how a small change can create ripples and how to deal with the science aspects of science fiction. We closed with a look at the idea of how to create a near-future science fiction world.

In the next chapter we'll look at the art of worldbuilding with a look at creating a future for humanity, including changes in technology and changes in where humans live. In later chapters we'll cover building entire new worlds and creating aliens to work within each world's parameters.

3 Worldbuilding for Terrans

Worldbuilding

Worldbuilding is the process of constructing an imaginary world, sometimes associated with a fictional universe.
Source: *Wikipedia*

- Approaching the art of worldbuilding
- Technology of the future
- Future weapons and future war
- Defining human cultures in other places
- Living quarters and entertainment
- The tricky question of religion in the future
- The future of humanity

In this chapter we are going to work on worldbuilding skills, which are probably some of the most important skills a science fiction writer can learn (along with how to write a very good story). Science fiction requires the ability to create believable worlds out of science fact and hypothesis, coupled with imagination. It must all work together.

Approaching the art of worldbuilding

Worldbuilding is an art form many new writers think they can skip if they set their story in the world they know. However, remember what I said in the introduction about horses and large cities and consider how changes will affect your future, even if you keep your story firmly grounded on Earth. The world changes with every new invention. So you must do worldbuilding for any science fiction story, including near-future tales. We have changed the Earth to suit us, and we will continue to change it, for better or worse, as long as we survive. Always consider how small changes ripple outwards to make larger changes in the pattern. So approach this element of writing with an open mind and don't be afraid to look at odd combinations; our world is filled with strange things which we somehow fit together to make a whole.

Some degree of worldbuilding comes naturally to all writers. As the story grows in the author's head, he sees the world with some of the details automatically sketched in. The author may not yet know why some areas work the way they do, however, he can see how various aspects of the world relate to the story. This is the easy part of worldbuilding. After all, a post-apocalyptic Earth would look far different from a utopian world, and a station on a world with a poisonous atmosphere would be far different from one placed on a terra-like world. As authors, we see the basics and direct our stories to fit into such a world and at the same time we create a world to fit the story we want to write.

Both physical and cultural worldbuilding are essential to making your story's background real enough to hold the reader's interest. As we have discussed, learning why things work as they do will add depth to your story. In this way, having a solid basis for your science fiction world will open unexpected doors and make your work more believable. A book's setting rarely remains static. Be prepared to add details to any place where your characters spend a good amount of time because the longer someone remains in one place, the more detail the character will notice in the setting. If the character is passing quickly from one place to another, however, the details will be blurred and can be painted with broader strokes.

Technology of the future

Science fiction is often defined by the level of technological change marking the setting as different from the world we know. That technology might be evident in spaceships moving throughout the solar system and beyond, or it might be something more down to earth. Technological changes in the world we know might come with the introduction of nanotechnology, true virtual reality machines, improvements in medicine, weather control, or many other transformations.

A few years ago, the burst of nanotechnology stories on the market nearly overwhelmed readers and it seemed as though nanotech became a common word overnight.

Today, while not quite as popular a theme as it was, nanotechnology is still a viable subject for science fiction. There are some real-world uses of nanotechnology already, but for science fiction this has gone beyond the idea of nano-sized particles to that of tiny machines. A nanotech machine is something built on the atomic and molecular scale, which means something about 100 nanometers or smaller. Such devices would be incredibly invasive and could be both helpful and harmful. The idea of nanotech machines to help in the medical profession, for example in clearing out choked arteries, destroying cancer cells and repairing internal damage, has fascinated people. But equally fascinating for the science fiction writer is what such machines could do in repairing the environment and fighting wars.

Similarly, the idea of virtual reality machines was formerly very popular in science fiction but has recently died down somewhat. This is ironic, since we seem to be moving closer to the real thing – but it may be that virtual reality is no longer futuristic enough to attract the attention it did a decade or so ago. Nonetheless, there are aspects of such stories which can still appeal to writers and readers, such as the idea of stepping outside reality into something fabricated, since being at the mercy of whatever controls the fabrication can lead to any number of adventures. What about virtual reality as a tool for the police, to recreate a crime scene and see what was possible? Virtual reality combined with artificial intelligence might be a way to recreate someone who is dead – having such a sage to call upon in times of need might make an interesting character. A number of stories have used virtual reality machines as spheres for entertainment, but as a writer you are not tied to what others have done, and the uses of such machines could range from education to punishment.

Nanotechnology is not the only change the future might bring when it comes to medicine, and some of the others might make equally interesting aspects of a future world. Improvements in medicines and diagnostic ability have dramatically changed the way some diseases are treated and have tamed others so they are not automatic death sentences. Problems and challenges arise with new medical systems, but if you imagine a future in which strides are continually made then you could expect the future to bring more medical miracles. But how about a future dealing with some of the more science fiction-related terms such as a 'fountain of youth' drug? Or some other way to secure immortality? Could people keep cloned body parts in case of emergencies? Could they clone themselves and raise them as children? Would there be some control on the birth rate? Changes in the world of medicine have already transformed our world, and are likely to continue to do so in the future. Everything from inoculations to what diseases are conquered (and what new ones appear) will affect the way in which people live.

Other technological changes could involve the weather and climate. The implications of a weather control system go far beyond making certain there are sunny days on the beach and snowpack in the mountains. If someone controlled the weather, they would control who is able to grow food. Most of the starvation in the world today revolves around droughts; if these could be controlled, then such technology could be a boon to people everywhere. However, such control could also lead to abuse. We have all seen the devastating effects of weather out of control, but how much worse could it be if people had the ability to direct hurricanes, tornadoes, floods and droughts against their enemies? Like many benevolent creations, the control of the weather could have disastrous results if it wasn't carefully monitored and controlled. People who create something cannot predict how it will be used or misused in the future.

What if...

Consider a scientific change and how it would impact some specific type of work – either an industry or community service – and what it would mean to the world. For instance, how would thieves behave if they knew that opening locks without the proper codes could release a small army of nano-bots to incapacitate them?

Future weapons and future war

The future of warfare is something that concerns and worries nearly everyone in the world today. We live in an age that combines some of the worst of all possibilities, from nuclear bombs to genetically-engineered viruses. Up until relatively recent times, warfare was mostly limited to the battle of one army against another but now no one is safe from the conflict.

How we fight in the future does not, based on our history of warfare so far, seem likely to be any more humane than it has ever been and it could be far more dangerous. We have the potential to wipe out humanity, or at the very least to knock civilization down to a level where it would be a long climb back up again. Humans are a dangerous breed and only our occasional good sense and survival instinct keep us from creating a situation from which there could be no return. Even Robert Oppenheimer, after the testing of nuclear weapons in New Mexico, had some reservations about what he had done. He said it best when he recited these lines from the Bhagavad Gita:

If the radiance of a thousand suns were to burst at once into the sky that would be like the splendor of the mighty one. Now I am become Death, the destroyer of worlds.

Small-scale weapons are always quickest to change and we've seen steady advances in pistols and other handguns since their invention. How they will change in the fictional future is up to the author. Laser or sonic pistols might be something to consider, though – as always – you will have to consider the power source required to keep such weapons functional. Along with such new weapons would most likely be the invention of protection against them, so start considering what sorts of shields might work as well.

Knives retain their basic form with small variations and it is unlikely they will undergo any drastic change in the future. While they might be considered an old-fashioned weapon, in some circumstances they could be more effective than projectile or light weapons. If domed colonies or ships didn't do away with weapons entirely, they might limit them to bladed weapons – and this could cause a resurgence in the use of swords for a perfectly logical reason.

Large-scale weapons, however, are likely to change as much or more than they already have. The fear of space-based weapon systems which could rain down destruction from orbit around the world is a valid worry. Long range missiles with nuclear or biological warheads are not something far-fetched. How does their existence change your story?

The future of war probably depends on what type of story you want to tell. Humans are argumentative and territorial, which is a bad combination. Individuals will sometimes pick fights and groups can often be caught up in what appears to be senseless violence. This has given humans a long history of warfare and this seems unlikely to stop though it might be diverted to other channels. If humanity found it was not alone in the galaxy, perhaps we might all band together against some new alien enemy, even without being certain of the aliens' intentions? Or would one human faction consider joining the aliens to gain an advantage?

Defining human cultures in other places

A walk through any busy downtown area of a large city will show you the variety of peoples living within the area as this is easy to guess by checking out the various ethnic restaurants. For humans, food is the most obvious area where a person of one culture will cross the cultural boundary into an exotic, new world. Holidays are also a link between people of different cultures.

When the writer creates a human settlement off-world, the culture often seems somewhat generic. This is sometimes done purposefully to show a future in which cultures have melded into a single form. However, consider how every time a group of humans breaks away from their homelands for any length of time, they adapt to where they are and create a new culture based on what has become important to their new lives. This process could take generations, but some of the changes might be evident in the first few years.

A writer can use this idea to create a new culture for the humans. A writer can also borrow from a prevalent culture if the particular cultural and ethnic group has a strong influence on a new settlement. Groups of people might migrate together to a new setting and this might include neighbours, family, a section of a population from a particular county, and so on.

A culture must be shared by a group of people (or aliens) and not simply be the eccentricity of a single person – though such a person might be the start of a cultural movement within a larger group. Consider, for instance, how much impact Elvis Presley had on the music world and how much, in turn, popular music changed the wider culture.

Humans adapt to new environments, which means they do more than simply find the best material to build their homes with – the new environment will affect them in other ways as well. An Englishman visiting parts of Mexico in the 1800s mistook the practice of a noon siesta as a sign of weakness in the inhabitants, brought on by their extremely spicy food, instead of what it really was – a cultural reaction to living in a desert where working in the extreme heat of the afternoon could be fatal. Such cultural misunderstandings are common. They can be easy to manufacture for a story if you prepare the groundwork with good, solid physical and cultural worldbuilding.

What if...

If your story includes different words and different places, what kinds of weapons would you expect your characters to take along? If there are no aliens in this fictional universe, are they worried about local animals? About other humans? What sort of defences would they build into their settlement in the case of one or the other?

Living quarters and entertainment

Once again, the purpose of your future location will have an important impact on the daily life of your characters and how they react within their world. For instance, living quarters and entertainment on spaceships or domed colonies is bound to be limited; in both cases, personal space might be something much sought after and given as a reward.

On a spaceship, there may be two types of people aboard – crew and passengers. Passengers may be people travelling on business (depending on the kind of space travel you have created) or emigrants heading to a new world. Such emigrants would rarely be rich and their quarters would most likely be little more than rooms with bunks.

Children, however, need room and so family groups might have a central 'play' area. Would women and children be confined to one area to ensure the children did not get into anything troublesome, with men and single women given more austere quarters? Could they all be expected to work in some way? Or is your new world importing something other than labourers or settlers, such as genetic diversity? Is the culture based around age groupings rather than gender? Do they value manipulation of symbols more than physical strength, making neither strength nor age the basis for positions of authority? Could children be the leaders in your culture? Perhaps much of the entertainment would take the form of training for the new world. The crew might find it important to help keep people busy and entertained because a large group of people with nothing to do can become a problem.

Ships which are filled only with crew, either as traders or military, might have much the same living arrangements but the entertainment would be aimed specifically at off-time activities and those might be geared more toward relaxing and private time. Or, if the ship is large enough, there might be some sort of contact sport event. Again, much of this depends on how large a ship, and how long a voyage, the crew is taking.

If your story begins with the group stepping out into their new world, how they got there and what they suffered along the way is going to play a part in the psychology of the people. It may remain an important factor a generation or two later, as they recall the horrors of the journey in history books.

A domed colony would face some of the same constrictions as a ship, however everyone there would have more of an interest in the location and activities than they might have had as passengers or crew on a ship.

Both living areas and entertainment might be drastically different on an open-air colony. Living quarters would be limited to building materials – but humans are good at adapting whatever is available to their needs. A first settlement might be filled mostly with barrack-type residences and only slow spread out into individual homes, if at all. If the world is dangerous, apartment complexes affording group protection might become the usual housing for families. If the world is primarily providing agricultural products, then housing would probably be spread out in single family units (or family groups and clans) and be individualistic, taking advantage of local resources.

A lot of the entertainment in such environments would be tied to the level of technology. Just because people came to this world by spaceship does not mean they will keep technology after they arrive. Power sources do not spring full-grown from the ground, neither do vehicles. Entertainment might become old-fashioned in many ways, such as storytelling, song festivals and sporting events. These activities might be used as reasons to get together and keep in contact and might be 'prospective mate' events as well.

The tricky question of religion and the future

Humans often have belief systems they can trace back several centuries. They hold to them in times of adversity and, although the beliefs mutate through the ages, they still represent a form of continuity linking generations together.

Splinter groups occur now and then but, overall, religion tends to be cohesive. So if your science fiction future has humans still closely tied to each other, then religion will play much the same role as it did when explorers found new areas of the Earth to settle. Some people will move to new areas and bring their beliefs with them. Others will move to new areas because they are members of a less popular group and they are looking for a place where they have more control over their lives. While religion has sometimes been a factor in emigration, it is not always the main reason. The Greek city states set up colonies of their own people both to relieve population pressure and to found settlements which would link back to the main city and bring in more riches.

If your human colonies have no direct ties back to Earth and the rest of humanity, their local religious ceremonies – followed by their beliefs – will most likely mutate to suit the needs of the new world. It's rare for people to all believe the same thing, either. If the group is religiously diverse, there might be some odd cross-pollination. If the religious elements of life are strong in your created community, then there will be people who feel the need to voice what they feel is wrong with the religion as it mutates and changes.

Creating an alien religion is a daunting task, unless the point is to make the religion echo human beliefs. Studying various religions can help you to pick out the different aspects of belief in general. Creating alien religious backgrounds has to be more than throwing together an interesting set of gods and having the aliens say the appropriate things when they pray or curse. Why they believe what they do and the history of their beliefs can be an important part of their culture. Or they may not have any religious beliefs at all. You do not have to make your aliens the same as your humans. Consider beyond the basics of what the aliens believe to who controls the religion and how an alien becomes a member – are they born to it, chosen by others, or tested in some way?

Religion can also have a strong impact on morals, etiquette and taboos. It can influence laws and education. It can be controlled by the rich and powerful or it can be the power of the poor. In human history, religion has been both a power for education and a haven for superstition. If you create a religion, look for both obtrusive and non-obtrusive ways to make it apparent. Holy buildings are obvious but place names can be used as well to define a piece of background. Plaza del Santo Palo indicates a far different background than Luther Place.

If you plan to make religion of any type a major part of your story, make certain you understand it, whether it is a real religion or one you are creating specifically for your book. This is a subject which cannot be approached in a haphazard manner if it is going to play an important part in your book. Even if you are writing about the religion you grew up with, learn as much about the history and technical side of how it is presented as possible. If, however, religion is not a major force in your story, don't spend too much time working on the details. Like everything else in the realm of worldbuilding, the point is to make certain you know enough for your specific needs.

Also consider what, if any, relationship there is between the religion in your world and the nature of that world. Religions may be influenced by seasons and celestial bodies – does your world have a significant detail that could have become incorporated? Holidays can be both religious and secular and can be important functions for your characters. In the past, important festivals took place at the time of planting and harvesting and if your colony has a need for groups of people to get together to perform some work on a regular basis, this is a good time to create a festival to go with it.

Mythology usually refers to past religious beliefs no longer considered valid and myths can play an important part in the history of your colonies or your aliens. We name things after myths, which have a universal appeal outside current religion. Answers to questions can sometimes be found in mythology after they have been lost to history. If you have a colony of humans who have been cut off from contact with the rest of humanity for a long time, they might have developed an interesting mythology about their own past. Writers can have a great deal of fun working with mythology, especially when they tie it into the history of the people. Myths can give clues about aspects of life the writer doesn't want to be obvious, but does want to have present so when the answer is made clear, the reader will realize it's been a part of the story all along.

> **What if...**
>
> Imagine a colony on another world, cut off from contact with Earth for at least five hundred years – or about ten generations because, obviously, they would not still be counting by Earth time. Or would they? How much of Earth culture do they still hold to? What might they change to adapt to their new world?

The future of humanity

The future you write about might include a human race that is very different from what we are now. Many science fiction tales are filled with mutations, clones and cyborgs as well as human-like inventions like androids, robots and computers with artificial intelligence.

Mutation is a normal part of the world and is how animals adapt and change. A natural mutation is something appearing within a group which spreads because it proves to be a better adaptation for survival. If the change is better for survival, the ones with this mutation are more likely to live long enough to mate and pass the mutation on to another generation and their natural mutation then spreads within the gene pool. The higher up the evolutionary scale an animal is, the longer it takes for a mutation to appear, so it is unlikely humans would naturally mutate in any significant way in a short time.

Mutation has been a two-sided sword for science fiction stories. It appears crudely as the bug-a-boo fear factor in the pulps and B-movies. But it also serves as a thought-provoking means by which science fiction writers can explore the potential of humanity in strange environments. Mutations can best be introduced if they are needed for some specific reason in the story. Larry Niven's *Integral Trees* has mutated humans who are adapted to move along the massive space-born trees of the story. Heinlein's *Orphans of the Sky* has a generation ship filled with mutations after an accident long past.

Cloning presents a different sort of problems to an author looking at a future society. The first is to find a legitimate reason to clone people. This might not be for the betterment of people but it needs to be a reason that will not have the reader asking why they bother. After all, humanity is incredibly prolific at reproducing and since we can neither feed nor care for all the humans on the world, creating clones for work purposes would be a useless waste of resources. The question of whether clones could be created for specific people, for instance cloning the Einsteins of the future, would depend on how much the author believed in inherited intelligence as opposed to environmental factors as being most crucial in influencing the development of intelligence.

Another question is whether humanity would want such 'special people' cloned to continue in whatever work they had been doing before? Or would this cause a kind of stagnation as the people looked only to previous geniuses and not to someone born in the new age?

Would humanity need clones for space exploration or colonization of worlds? That depends a great deal on both how you create your future Earth and how many worlds need to be colonized. Humans tend to like adventure and exploration and, with a world already burdened with overpopulation, finding people willing to make a new start might not be difficult. On the other hand, if the 'new start' is for a future generation (that is, if at least one generational group will grow old and die in transit) it might be harder to find enough altruistic people to take on the journey.

Would clones be used strictly for the type of work others no longer do, making them a slave population? This might not only be dirty, demeaning grunt work but also military and space exploration might have ranks of clones for especially dangerous work. But how trustworthy would those clones be?

Who would supply the genetic material for clones? Could people clone themselves for medical reasons, to supply their own body parts in case of emergencies? Or grow a younger version of themselves and transplant the brain when the original body grows old?

Cloning of humans always raises ethical and religious questions. There is probably never going to be a consensus where questions of religion and science overlap, so a future with cloning is bound to bring conflict on this level as well. Consider such problems when you are creating your population's religion. If you are going to write a book dealing with the concept of clones, don't overlook the possibility of adding more conflict to your story through this avenue.

One book dealing with the cloning of a famous figure was *Joshua Son of None* by Nancy Freedman which dealt a great deal with trying to recreate the experiences of the former life in hopes of generating an exact duplicate. C. J. Cherryh's *Cyteen* deals with many aspects of cloning in a science fiction setting, as do some of her other works including *Forty Thousand in Gehenna*. Not only does she deal with the how and why of cloning, but also with the ethical aspects of manipulating people for specific gains.

Cyborgs are a symbiosis of living and artificial life systems and are sometimes used in fiction as a way to question what it means to be human and where we can draw the line. They are the bridge between humanity and technology and deal with technology in ways a normal human could not. A badly injured person might become cybernetic in composition, their human body being augmented by technology, as in Michael Caiden's Cyborg: A Novel, which was the inspiration for the *Six Million Dollar Man* television series. In other cases, a person might keep a cyborg to do specific jobs, such as the character of Braedee, the chief of Centauri Corporate Security, in *Catspaw* by Joan D. Vinge. In the latter case, society would need a compelling reason to allow such augmentation, which would set the cyborgs apart from other humans. Anything which made one group into 'super-humans' would be bound to draw resentment and distrust from the others. The idea of being part machine also leads to questions about where humanity ends and machine begins, as well as the larger question of what it means to be human in itself.

From cyborgs we move to androids, which are fully mechanical but shaped to look like humans and are often created to mimic human thought and action. This takes the question of 'humanity' one step further, prompting questions about how much of our actions dictate what we are. Isaac Asimov's famous *I, Robot* collection of short stories is one look into the world of androids. The story *Runaround* from this collection also includes Asimov's famous Three Laws of Robotics:

1. A robot may not injure a human being or, through inaction, allow a human being to come to harm.

2. A robot must obey orders given to it by human beings, except where such orders would conflict with the First Law.

3. A robot must protect its own existence as long as such protection does not conflict with the First or Second Law.

Philip K. Dick ignored such 'rules' for his book *Do Androids Dream of Electric Sheep?* (made into the movie *Blade Runner*) and thereby put the humans and androids on a collision course.

Androids might work well as warriors, household workers, guards and companions – anywhere a human-shaped creation might prove aesthetically preferable to a machine looking like a machine. Honda's ASIMO humanoid robot shows considerable real-world progress in this field.

While androids are robots in essence, not all robots are androids. A robot, in the larger sense, is any device which is computer-controlled to perform actions. Robots which are not humanoid in appearance form the line where we begin to move from the androids of fictional works and into the real world of today's mechanical constructs. The working robots of today are shaped to do the job and are often used for dangerous or for repetitive work. They are becoming increasingly multifaceted as computers become more complex and generate the ability for finer control.

Computers, with or without a robotic body, form another borderline between fictional stories and real-world applications. Computers are increasingly powerful and capable of complex calculations and can sometimes mimic human decision. However, the search for artificial intelligence takes us back into the realm of science fiction. The AI computers of science fiction come in various forms, including the famous HAL 9000 of Arthur C. Clarke's *2001: A Space Odyssey* and Mike from Robert Heinlein's *The Moon is a Harsh Mistress*.

AI computers, whether housed in android shapes or in plain black boxes, again prompt the question of the sentient threshold and what it means to be living and conscious of the world. The AI computers of the fictional world are essentially human in thought, though super-human in ability. They present another form of 'humans' which can be used in science fiction.

What if...

What kind of world could you imagine in which androids did all the physical work, leaving humans to enjoy art and recreation? Would humans begin to vie for creative honours? Would sports become more dominant in society? Would humans be paid for their art and sports participation, or would they own androids and collect payment for work done by them? Would the androids need overseers of some sort and, if so, would this be a highly sought-after job or one considered to be the bottom of the ladder to success?

In this chapter we looked at how to take the first steps in worldbuilding by defining a future which is closely related to human culture and technology, and also how science will have affected the future.

In the next chapter, we'll look at the technical side of creating whole worlds including the author's choice of star types, gravity parameters, and more.

4 Building New Worlds

- Worldbuilding: the wide view
- The stars
- The worlds
- Understanding biomes
- Alien weather

In this chapter, we'll look at some of the fundamentals of creating whole worlds, from choosing the right sun to looking at biomes as they apply to Earth. Creating worlds in science fiction takes more than dropping a world and a couple of moons into place. This requires a bit of scientific knowledge and a lot of imagination.

Worldbuilding: the wide view

Creating a world – or a group of worlds – for a science fiction story begins with understanding how our world works. Textbooks on physical geography, meteorology, geology, oceanography and any other subject dealing with the planetary sciences are very beneficial to science fiction writers. Add in astronomy and cosmology to see how other worlds differ, especially if you do not intend to take Earth with you to a new settlement. A book like the wonderful *A Traveler's Guide to Mars* by William K. Hartmann can provide you with fantastic details for any Mars-like world. This is a great look at an alien world.

Another book to try is *Welcome to Moonbase* by Ben Bova. This book is set up like a guide book to a settlement on the moon, providing information on manufacturing, living quarters and more. It is a great resource for any sort of domed colony you might create.

You can also find books on spaceship and space station design, both theoretical and real. Look for works on other subjects you will deal with in your science fiction tale. Textbooks can often be bought at used bookstores and college outlets. Keep some basic information books on hand because you will inevitably want to look up something when the local library is closed.

Science magazines are a fount of inspiration, too. If you can't afford subscriptions, make a habit of going to the library and reading the current issues or seeing if they have an online version. Be sure to take copious notes or photocopy some of the work!

The Internet is a good reference tool only if you use it wisely and realize anyone can state something as though it is a fact, even if they don't know what they're talking about. Double check all information you gather from websites, especially if they are not affiliated with a college or university.

The stars

Understanding the basics of how stars are categorized will help you set your story beyond the solar system. While you might write stories based on super giants, white dwarfs and black holes, the majority of stories focusing on either Earth-settled worlds or worlds with Earth-like life forms are going to take place within a narrow range of 'main sequence' stars.

Main sequence stars, which are predominant in our galaxy, are powered by the fusion of hydrogen and helium within their cores. The mass of the star dictates its lifespan and luminosity. The greater the mass, the stronger the gravitational pull inward, but as the gas compresses it exerts pressure in the opposite direction (which would not be enough to overcome the gravity without the added radiation pressure of the hydrogen). These stars are usually very stable and we see little change in them over extremely long periods of time.

Mass and luminosity are linked, which makes it relatively easy to place a star within the main sequence listing. The lowest mass a main sequence star could have is about 0.08 times the mass of our sun; below this mass threshold, a star cannot generate the temperature to fuse hydrogen and slips into the realm of a brown dwarf. Usually, a larger star has a brighter luminosity and a higher mass, which puts it higher on the main sequence listing. The higher mass for a main sequence star is somewhere around 200 times the size of our sun, which makes them very bright but, because their higher mass makes their core hotter, they burn out faster than a star with lower mass. An estimate of our sun's lifespan in its current stage is about 10 billion years, while a high mass star might burn out in only 20 million years (meaning that even if it had a planetary system, intelligent life would not have time to evolve there).

Stars are generally referred to by their spectral classifications, which are given in letters:

- O Apparent colour is blue and they have a temperature range of 30,000 to 60,000 degrees Kelvin
- B Apparent colour is blue-white and they have a temperature range of 10,000 to 30,000 degrees Kelvin
- A Apparent colour is white and they have a temperature range of 7,500 to 10,000 degrees Kelvin
- F Apparent colour is white and they have a temperature range of 6,000 to 7,500 degrees Kelvin
- G Apparent colour is yellowish-white and they have a temperature range of 5,000 to 6,000 degrees Kelvin
- K Apparent colour is yellow-orange and they have a temperature range of 3,500 to 5,000 degrees Kelvin
- M Apparent colour is orange to red and they have a temperature range of 2,000 to 3,500 degrees Kelvin

(There is a very simple way to remember the spectral sequence: **O**h **B**e **A** **F**ine **G**irl/**G**uy, **K**iss **M**e.)

Each of these letter designations is followed by a numerical system of 0–9, with 0 being the hottest, brightest stars within the group and 9 the coolest, dimmest stars. This is a very easy way to track the main types of stars. Our sun is a G2 which is fairly hot, yellow and bright.

Over 76 per cent of all stars in the main sequence are M-class stars. The types of stars which could possibly support an Earth-like world, however, would fall in the F, G and K ranges, which make up about 22 per cent of the stars in our galaxy. Since there are about 100 billion stars in our galaxy, this means about 22 billion stars could possibly support Earth-like populations.

This gives the science fiction writer a very large playground. In order for a planet to be viable, it must be within a certain distance of its sun based on the star's size, brightness and the amount of radiation it puts out. The hotter and brighter the sun, the farther away an Earth-like world must be.

What if...

Stars seem to have long lives from the point of view of a normal human lifespan but how would that impression change if your characters had unlimited lifetimes? What sort of civilization could they create? How would they move it from world to world as their suns died? What would the sky look like under an alien sun? Try to imagine a world under a number of different star types and how a star's colour and size would affect what a person would see. Is the world on which you stand Earth-like or alien? Is the atmosphere of the world thin and clear, or thick and soupy? What are the sunsets like? How does this impact your story, or your characters?

The worlds

Once you have your star itself figured out, there are other parameters to take into account. Its path around the sun, axial tilt and all those things that go into making the Earth year are factors you need to consider. You also need to consider whether or not your new world is going to have a moon or two. Some theories contend that life could not have existed on Earth without the movement of the tides, and these are controlled almost entirely by the moon.

Gravity is an effect of mass, which needs to be remembered when creating a sun for your fictional setting. For an Earth-like planet, the safe range of gravity would be about between 70 per cent and 150 per cent of Earth's gravity.

If you are doing a story based on Earth or in an Earth-like setting, find information on the type of areas that can serve as settings and study them. Forests are more than trees and deer, and deserts are more than sand and snakes. Do you know the difference between savannah and grasslands or what factors create deserts? The Gobi desert, for instance, is far from the equator – it is worth understanding what factors created it and how they differ from the Sahara desert's creation.

Learn about the flora, fauna, geology and climate of different settings. The more you know about what goes into the creation of each type, the more you can add to make the place come alive in unexpected, but real, ways. Also, no world is all one type; even desert worlds will have polar caps and jungle worlds will have equatorial hot spots. Knowing such areas exist can help expand your fictional world from a narrow swatch of land to a full, alien setting.

The same is true if you are building a space station. There will be more to such a place than plain steel walls. Study ocean liners, old sailing ships and buildings in hostile environments. Humanity has often created multiple answers for any single problem when it comes to habitation, so take advantage of this knowledge to create something unique but functional.

Research is only half the key to successful worldbuilding, though. The other half is, of course, imagination. If you are writing a story placed in a desert, studying of the Sahara might help, or the Gobi or Death Valley. However, unless you intend to place the story in a specific real-world location, don't be afraid to experiment.

Understanding biomes

Understanding biomes, either to draw from the ones on Earth for your story or to create viable biomes for a new world, is important to most science fiction stories. Most writers deal with this section instinctively. They know there are no alligators in the Arctic regions and they'll feel safe creating long-haired creatures for their alien world's snow land. However, the more you understand about the diversity of a biome, the more realistic you can make your setting. This can be especially important in any story about terra-forming a planet, where the balance of life forms is essential if your work is to be effective and self-sustaining.

Biomes, or habitats, are interactive areas, where everything within the system reacts to what else is present. From life to death, the system has to be balanced in order for it to work properly. We have all read tales of things out of balance, like the introduction of animals into areas where they have no natural predators. You can use such knowledge to your advantage, or it can be the little piece you overlook when you write your book. It's better to know all the pieces, though you may not actively use them, rather than missing out something which could create a problem later requiring you to do a retro-fix throughout the story.

Also remember your readers have to suspend their disbelief to read science fiction. If you create situations they know can't work, they will have to make an effort to continue reading the story. Disrupt their reading too often and they'll not only stop reading, they'll be blogging about this terrible science fiction story!

Biomes come in several types and extend over large sections, forming relatively stable areas. They range from Arctic tundra to desert wastelands, with several types of grasslands, forests, tropical and marine areas as well. Within these spheres, everything, from microbes to plants to predators, lives in equilibrium. When anything is upset, then trouble spreads within the system. If the weather changes, plants might fail and this would lead to the death of the animals which live on those plants, and then in turn the deaths of the animals which live on those animals.

It is a very delicate balance, and creating a total system for a world, whether totally alien or terra-formed, would be impossible for a writer, at least if the author ever hoped to actually write the book to go with it. We are lucky, however, because all we need to do is see the broader picture, add in some of the key types of creatures and plants, and be aware of what things would not happen in such a system. Once again let me remind you, though, that no world is entirely one biome. Also, if you have a world that has inhabitants that are Earth-like, then it has to have an Earth-like structure to go with it.

According to *Van Nostrand's Scientific Encyclopedia* there are eleven basic biomes:

1. Deserts
2. Tundra
3. Grasslands
4. Savannah
5. Chaparral
6. Woodland
7. Coniferous forest
8. Deciduous forest
9. Tropical forest
10. Reefs
11. Rocky shores

Each of these areas has its own weather, animal life and special needs. There will also be border areas between some of the biomes. Quite obviously, biomes are not controlled by political borders but rather by natural obstacles like mountains and oceans.

The study of how nature works on Earth will help you create a believable world of your own. Learning as much as you can about any subject which catches your interest will make you a better writer. Authors are often told to write about what they know. It would be better, however, to say to write about what you are willing to learn. You do not have to know everything about the sciences needed to understand how nature works, but you have to be willing to learn enough to make wise, logical decisions.

A science fiction writer can't afford to be complacent about his creations or to be unwilling to learn the material which will help create a better novel.

> **What if...**
>
> What if you intended to write a story based primarily in a desert? What factors would be important to the setting? What about a story placed in a tundra setting? What could you do to make either type of setting seem more alien?

Alien weather

All worlds will have weather patterns and these are affected by many factors including moisture, bodies of liquid, rotation, gravity, solar energy and land masses. The easiest way to make decisions about your own alien weather is to understand how weather systems work on Earth. A few hours with the Weather Channel or on a weather website will give you some idea, but studying a book or two can also help. The *Audubon Society Field Guide to North American Weather* has several introduction pages which apply to weather all over the world and these can help in looking at how the larger systems work.

The Earth's atmosphere is made up of several layers. If you started at the top and worked down to the ground they would be:

Ionosphere
Thermosphere
Mesosphere
Stratosphere
Troposphere

You can use a similar model for your new world. Weather takes place in the troposphere which varies in thickness from about five miles at the poles to twelve miles at the equator and it is within this narrow band that weather is created on Earth. The ionosphere, on the other hand, is important to Earth in an odd way: the ionized (electrified) molecules in this layer form because they absorb radiation from the sun which creates a sort of mirror allowing us to bounce radio waves from one part of the world to another. The aurora borealis also takes place in the ionosphere, caused by solar flares.

Below is a very simplistic view of how some of the more obvious aspects of weather work, but there are so many other factors which actually come into play that it would take an entire book of its own to cover them all. However, having a basic understanding of weather factors can help an author create suitable systems and 'predict' weather on an alien world. Further study of the science of weather will enhance this ability and give you further control over your new world.

One basic weather factor is the wind. At the very basic level, when the Earth rotates it causes air masses to move so that they curl away from the equator. In the northern hemisphere, the air rotates to the right and in the southern hemisphere it rotates to the left. This effect works with atmospheric pressure to help create winds. There are several prevailing wind systems in the world, which include the westerlies, northeast trade winds, southeast trade winds and polar easterlies. These have tremendous impact on weather and, as some of the names indicate, on early shipping and trade practices. If your alien world is in the age of space travel, they had a past just as Earth has had one and knowing something like the pattern of the winds could be important in some instances. It could also be important to someone visiting.

Another basic weather factor is the sun. Solar energy works to evaporate liquid into the atmosphere. Because the sun strikes a larger area around the equator, this air is heated more evenly and a great amount of moisture moves into the atmosphere. Here the winds begin to disperse the moisture out over the upper and lower latitudes. As the moisture moves away from the equator it cools, and forms into clouds.

Clouds come in so many different forms there are thick field guides to help identify the various cloud formations and the weather they produce. From altostratus to ground fog, our world is filled with the ever-changing shape of clouds and the dangerous weather some of them portend.

The weather's cooling mechanisms come in a number of ways. As warm, moist air forms at the ground, it is sometimes lifted by air currents which are themselves formed by the uneven heating of different areas of ground. As the moist air rises, it cools and when it reaches the dew point it starts condensing into small drops and form into clouds. If they continue to condense they will become heavy enough to rain.

If moist air is pushed upward by a mountain, it will also condense. This is called orographic lifting and it is one of the chief triggers for the Indian monsoons as the moisture from the ocean comes across land and hits the Himalayas and releases a tremendous amount of rain. Warm air can also be forced upward when it meets a strong cold front and this will also cause condensation.

Destructive storms are sometimes formed by the collision of cold and warm fronts. Cold air is dryer than warm air, which is able to hold water vapor without it condensing. When a cold front moves through, the weather will be cooler and generally less cloudy.

An important factor to creating snow and ice is the presence of small dust particles in the air, around which water begins to condense. A powerful snow storm also needs a steady inflow of moisture.

Hurricanes need relatively shallow, warm water to grow into dangerous storms and once they move inland, they begin to weaken, though the first blows can be devastating.

So by this it is easy to see how terrain has a serious effect on weather patterns. In some cases, high mountains stop virtually all moisture from moving past them so deserts form in the leeside while seasonal flooding occurs on the windward side. Even on the relatively small Hawaiian Islands there is a considerable difference in rainfall from the windward to the leeward sides of the islands.

The typical tornado in the American Midwest forms when moisture-laden air from the Gulf of Mexico moves northward and collides with the extremely cold, Arctic air moving southward across Canada. When the two collide, the extreme difference in temperature causes both condensation and chaotic winds. Sometimes these winds rotate and become funnel clouds which, if they drop to the ground become a tornado. This is an example of the importance of understanding the circumstances caused by geography: the North American Midwest is 40 times more likely to have a tornado than Great Britain, and 100 times more likely than Africa.

Weather features in our everyday life and it should be the same for an alien world, no matter whether you create destructive storms or not. Humans accept weather as part of life and though we may not often think about it in scientific terms, we do remain aware of what is going on around us. Soft breezes and deadly winds, gentle rains and devastating floods – they are all part of our lives. Ignoring weather on alien worlds is only limiting some of the most important and easily manipulated material which will help you define the world, give it depth and create problems that will interest your reader.

What if...

What if you created a world with stronger gravity: how would this affect the rising moisture and condensation? Since a heavier gravity might also mean fewer mountain ranges, this could also affect cloud formation. Would this mean most life would concentrate near large bodies of water (or other liquid) where evaporation and condensation would occur within a narrow band? What would this mean for your characters and for the flora and fauna of their world?

In this chapter we looked at the very basics of creating a fictional world from choosing the right beginnings to understanding the basics of gravity, biomes and weather. By further experimentation and studying the various aspects of a world you can create something which will not only be unique but will also remain logically grounded in its foundations.

The next chapter will deal with the creation of aliens to populate strange worlds, how to rationally make them fit their world, and how to fit their culture to their world and their special needs.

5 Extra Arms Do Not Make an Alien

Building your *others*

- Defining *their* world
- Extra arms and wings
- Some aliens are more alien than others
- One thing leads to another
- Technology, form and culture
- The daily life of aliens
- Naming aliens

The heart of science fiction is worldbuilding, which includes creating aliens as well as strange worlds. This work requires forethought, research and a willingness to look beyond the superficial. In this section, we'll look at some of the ways in which you can define and create aliens. Some of the material, especially in the area of culture, can also be adapted to define humans in a new environment.

Deciding how 'non-human' you want your creatures to be will help to determine the influences you use to create them. The age of simplistic bug-eyed monsters is past. Your aliens must have a reason for how they look and what they do.

Defining *their* world

Humans and all other creatures on Earth are adapted to this world. Most animals are also adapted to their environment, but humans are different. We can live in many different lands and climates specifically because we do not have to physically adapt to them. Instead, we create things – buildings for shelter, farm equipment to grow our own food – rather than having to depend on what is in the environment.

This is a very important aspect of creating aliens. If you want aliens who are like humans, then they must come from a similar background such as a terra-compatible world. In this way, you will make use of something commonly known as convergent evolution. Simply put, this means that organisms which are not related to each other may take a similar form if they have a similar habitat. Camels and llamas look somewhat alike, for instance, because they occupy the same sort of niche but in two different continents. In other cases, living creatures have taken on comparable form or colouring which helps them survive in a similar habitat. The wings of insects, birds and bats all developed independently in order to perform the same function.

In some cases, these animals had a common ancestor in prehistoric times, which is something a science fiction writer can consider as well. Were all the worlds peopled from one source? Are all the animals much the same, too?

This doesn't mean the world has to be exactly like Earth, or that the aliens must be identical to humans. However, if you want similar beings you need to remain within some strict parameters. The world itself would need to fall within a narrow range of factors including star-type, world size, temperature range, available minerals and water content. The combination of factors favouring life on Earth is complex and includes everything that makes up the atmosphere, hydrosphere, lithosphere and biosphere. Diverge drastically outside of Earth's parameters in any of these areas and you are bound to step outside the realm of Earth-compatible, which means aliens would not be human-like – though you might still create something unusual.

Non-human-like aliens have their draw, of course. However, they do not demand any less understanding of the factors which go into making a human-like alien. Before you can understand your aliens, you must understand their world. Once you have defined the parameters of where the aliens began life, you can start looking at the reasonable adaptations which would fit into such a world. Or you can do it the other way around – define what you want in your aliens and then fit the world to what you want.

There are several aspects of an alien world which need to be defined. The first thing you have to decide is how close to human you want your aliens to be. This does not mean they have to look like humans but if you want humans and the aliens to interact on some level, they must have some sort of common ground on which they can find a way to communicate. The aliens are going to have to come from a sort of world which would create a creature able to interface with humans. There have been stories where beings vastly different from humans interact via computers, but if the aliens are too different would they have such devices?

Aside from placing the world in the right type of star system (see the previous chapter) the next important influence is gravity. Gravity will affect not only the structure of your aliens themselves but also the shape of the land masses and the structure of the atmosphere. There are a few simple ideas to keep in mind: stronger gravity means lower land forms (no high mountain ranges) and a thicker atmosphere at the ground level. This would mean a world with few or no tides, plants would not grow very tall and weather patterns would be affected as well. Flying creatures like birds could probably not exist as they can only fly on Earth because of their hollow bone structures, which would be too fragile to work on a planet with heavier gravity.

There are some parameters you can juggle – you can make a world a little heavier than Earth or all the way up to about 1.5 times the Earth's gravity if you want your inhabitants to stay close to human-like, as something weighing 100 pounds on Earth would weigh 150 pounds on the new world. And what of the appearance of the aliens? They would most likely be squat and thick-boned. A heavier atmosphere would also mean a different breathing system and probably a rougher skin. Eye structure might be different, especially if the aliens do not have a reason to look upward – remember, there are no flying creatures and no tall trees. Also, humans see in colour because we have cones and rods in our eyes. Rods are more numerous but it is the cones that process colours. But many animals on Earth, especially nocturnal ones, don't see in colour. So if your world has less daylight it might be that colour receptors in its inhabitants' eyes would not have developed.

By contrast, a planet with lower gravity than Earth would have a different effect. It might be populated with light-boned, tall aliens. Flying creatures, or creatures like flying squirrels which actually glide rather than fly, might be common. The world would be filled with tall things – mountains and plants – and would have a thin atmosphere.

If the author has specific ideas about aliens, it will be helpful to consider what sort of world would best create such a creature, though the world will have many different types of climate. Earth is filled with everything from deadly hot sandy deserts to equally deadly freezing snow-covered lands. Your beings will have evolved in one area and spread to others, at least if they are anything like humans. Or perhaps not. Perhaps some basic life forms might be linked to specific environments. These are your aliens – you need only make them work logically within your creation.

What if...

The lowlands of a new world are filled with thick fetid air, much of it poisonous to humans. The liquid has gathered at the bottom of this heavy world and is viscous and acidic. The visitors do not expect to find life...but an exploration team does find something. What would they find? What would the world be like in general to create such a situation and creatures?

Extra arms and wings

If the author wanted intelligent aliens with multiple arms, those arms would need to have a reason for existence. A world where climbing skills are essential could make multiple arms important for staying connected to safety, much as prehensile tails work for some animals in wooded areas. So including wooded areas or craggy mountains might help create a credible world for such climbing aliens. It would not be the only defining environmental feature, but it would be part of their world.

Consider how different a spaceship or other living quarters would be for beings who have multiple limbs and who are used to climbing rather than walking. Ceilings and floors would probably not be any different than any other wall but passageways could be covered with bars and nets to afford easy grabbing places.

What about wings? Again, a primary consideration would be gravity. It can't be too light or else you won't have the dynamics needed to make the aliens human-like. This means the aliens will have to make other adaptations. A lighter gravity does mean a less dense atmosphere and a narrower band of viable living space. For example, high mountains (which could be common because gravity is not pulling them back down) might be without atmosphere at their higher peaks. Within the biosphere, plant life would tend to grow tall and thin since it wouldn't need a lot of support. So would this require their ships and living areas to be full of large, wide areas?

Any basic change you make from the human form to the alien needs a reason and also needs to be followed through into the world in which they exist. If an alien species had a reptilian-like skin because of a corrosive atmosphere, then they would need protection for things like eyes as well. And how would they do that in an Earth-like atmosphere? Would the oxygen level be too rich?

This brings up another, very important aspect of your human-like aliens and humans. How do they actually interact? What is the common ground where they can meet? Can they ever truly come face-to-face, or is there always some eco-system barrier between them?

One way to help imagine aliens is to study some of the stranger creatures of Earth. A trip to a zoo or aquarium, especially with a camera in hand, can help. So can reading books about animal behaviour. Be open to what you read and look beyond the idea of animals. For instance, according to *Grzimek's Animal Life Encyclopedia*, North American prairie dogs do something unusual in the animal kingdom: when the young come of age, the older generation leave the burrow and build new burrows along the edge of the territory so that the younger, less experienced animals have the safer area. Something like this could be an important defining characteristic for an alien race.

If you work at it, you can make very nearly any kind of intelligent alien. The trick is to make the aliens work within the confines of their world so you understand as much about them as possible before you move them anywhere else.

> **What if...**
>
> If a world had intelligent creatures with six limbs, how would they move? What would they use those limbs for when they were not climbing? How would having so many limbs affect their balance, the placement of their head (or whatever is the equivalent to it) and how they literally view the world?

Some aliens are more alien than others

If you are creating a story with aliens who are not human-like, you still need to look at the dynamics of the world where they came into existence. What will change, though, is how they interact with humans, if they do so at all. Aliens born of a methane environment could be so entirely different from humans that there is no way for the two species to connect. By the same token, this means they are unlikely to have much of the same interests, either, and might only meet in passing.

Some aliens might be intermediate between human and something too alien to deal with. The interaction with such beings would likely be very difficult and filled with misunderstandings and unforeseen dangers as the aliens react in ways the humans did not expect. Such beings could be used as a sort of 'wild card' player in the story, creating havoc at unexpected times. The author would need to know the reasons for such actions, of course, but they could appear random and unpredictable to the characters of the book since they would not have the author's special knowledge. There may be a time when one of the characters figures out a pattern but, for the most part, the aliens could be something unknown and unknowable, adding to the feeling there is more in the universe than humans.

Whatever type of alien you create, build them through a series of careful steps and make certain the aliens work within the parameters you have set. Think outside the box when it comes to aliens and see if you can find different motivations and triggers so they can be more than humans in new skins. It will pay off in a richer, more exotic story.

One thing leads to another

Creating the geology and plant life for a new world does not tell you how your characters are going to interact with them. Worldbuilding is far more than mapmaking or creating everything for the environment. When it comes to the story, you need to see how people (human or alien) would utilize the resources available to them. The most extravagant and detailed worldbuilding will not create a good story. You must put it to practical use, and how resources are used becomes the culture of the group.

What other sorts of things need to go into a culture? Creating a culture can include everything from religion to housing, from marriage rites to burial rites, and from music to literature. Taboos, myths and legends are a large part of culture and can be fertile ground for explaining odd changes.

Just as a small change in the real world can have a ripple effect on our society, everything you create for the basics of your alien world will affect everything else. We've already seen how something as basic as gravity will affect the shape and size of your people. Let's look at some basics which can apply not only to aliens but also to human groups living on alien worlds.

We can start with the basics of habitat, which is the natural environment surrounding the group. Is the area in which the story takes place a desert region? Why did they settle there rather than at the polar regions where they are more likely to find ice, or the mid-latitudes where there would most likely be a better climate? You can find an answer if you want one, but make certain it is plausible within the confines of your story universe. For instance, a settlement in the midst of an inhospitable desert might be made for the sake of a mining centre. Another group might settle at the polar regions because of the abundance of moisture: humans need water and if you have created humanoid aliens, there's no reason they can't have the same needs and limitations.

An important factor is the degree of competition for habitable environments at an important stage in the evolution of the aliens. If any creature finds a spot where it is comfortable, it will have no reason to change and move on. Most creatures on Earth have found their niche and cannot exist outside it. For example, reptiles need a warm environment. They cannot exist in the icy lands of the north because they are cold-blooded and need a certain amount of heat in order to keep their body functioning. Warm-blooded creatures, however, do not need an external heat source for normal activity and tend to spread farther.

Habitat influences three very important factors: shelter, clothing and food. If the habitat was mild, shelter buildings could be less substantial and made mostly to stand up to dangerous creatures or occasional storms. They could be easily built from local resources and be simple to replace. But if the local habitat was harsh, then buildings serve as protection against the elements and survival depends on the structures being well-made. Building materials may not be locally available, which means building becomes a cooperative effort of some sort. A single, larger building might be easier to build and maintain than several small ones, this would affect how the people within it live, making for a more communal society as a whole.

Clothing and skin types are important aspects of habitat. When creating aliens, the type of habitat where they first evolved will be an important factor in the type of innate covering they have, whether it be skin like humans, or fur or scales. On Earth, many of the fur-bearing animals evolved during the last ice age and spread outward, so they are now in areas, like steaming jungles, where you would not expect to find fur-coverings.

Habitat also affects food sources. If the habitat is mild, food is usually easy to acquire. This affects the pace of life in general, since the drive to get enough to eat is not the primary need of the community. However, such areas are often teeming with life, and protection against enemies and defending food supplies could be important.

In some human societies, women became the gatherers and men the hunters. This is because women are the ones who defend, protect and raise the young, who are both vulnerable and difficult to move in a time of danger. Women are perfectly capable of hunting, as many have proven down through the ages. But from a practical point of view it is far safer for them to gather non-moving supplies (seeds from plants, garden vegetables, eggs from wild and domestic fowl) than it is for them to pack up a child or two and go hunting for game which might be dangerous and certainly needs stealth and quiet – qualities children are not likely to have.

However, this does not mean an alien society must follow the same path. There are alternatives, including younger women hunting, older people staying with the young, age groups of both sexes involved in certain types of work such as hunting, gathering, child care, building, warriors, etc. So you can experiment with what we know about the human race to create something different for both aliens and human societies which are no longer tied to Earth.

Defending food supplies in a harsh environment is also important, especially where there will be a lot of competition for those foods. In an environment where abundant plant life is lacking, such as deserts and snow fields, hunting will become all the more important.

When a small group of hunters brings in a limited amount of food supplies, distribution becomes an important aspect of life. This, in turn, creates a rank system within the society and sometimes the start of a barter system, where clothing or cooking supplies might be traded for the food items. Barter can lead to a money system, where a form of riches is traded rather than an item needed for survival. Both barter and money systems can lead to a wide discrepancy between the haves and have-nots.

Rank systems in a society also lead to rules of behaviour and etiquette towards others and can have a profound influence on who is allowed to mate with whom. If someone is in charge, that person has to be accorded a special kind of respect which is not given to others who rank lower. This sign of respect may go no farther than allowing the person first choice in foods, or it may be present in all aspects of life. This behaviour is also passed down through the rank lines in various degrees. It does not mean those above are cruel or rude to those below, however. A society could be inherently polite toward all, but still have a rank system.

A rank system might be the start of a family genealogy and myths which gradually expand and give the reason why certain groups are in charge down through the ages. Knowledge can also be hoarded to form a rank system, so certain people who know how to do something important to the group as a whole are accorded a higher station.

Etiquette and morals are linked, and morals sometimes influence clothing styles as well. Religion can also have an impact on all three, and influence knowledge (including what is allowed to be known) as well.

Make the types of creatures on your world diverse. Earth has more than just humans and there is no reason to limit some other world to one or two different creatures. They are all going to be part of the world's cultural interaction as well, whether as food sources or dangerous enemies. From microbes to huge animals, they can all have a place on your world.

Nothing stands alone in a society and if you look closely at all the pieces you put together, you will see the pattern of how they affect one another. Anything I've presented here can be changed and adapted to create an entirely different society. Adding in the diversity that makes up an alien race will also change the entire society, whether those changes are in body forms, genders, or anything else you might consider.

What if...

If you create a world which is not quite Earth-like and people it with alien creatures, what sort of senses would native beings evolve? We have five senses and we rely on them to give us information about the world around us, with reactions ranging from too bright to too cold. Could there be other senses?

Technology, form and culture

Technology is a large part of culture. We sometimes define cultures by their level of technology using terms ranging from Stone Age to Industrial Age. The less human-like your new races are, the less human-like their technology will be as well. Technology means anything which is used as a tool. Computers are part of technology but so are rakes. Rocks shaped to work wood and hide are tools and part of technology and so are laser beams used to cut holes in metal.

Earth is still filled with people at different technological levels, even in this age where it seems we are all so closely connected. In the past, such differences were far more noticeable. When the Europeans arrived in North American, they found a Paleolithic (Stone Age) native culture. This had a devastating effect on the relationship between the two groups of peoples since the native people had no real defence against the better technology of the Europeans. So don't forget to take into account the differences in technological development between one group and another when they come into contact.

Furthermore, technology and body shape are intertwined. An alien hammer might not look like a hammer to humans, who are used to something with a handle to grasp and a heavy weight on the end. Would, for instance, winged aliens have something they drop rather than propel with their own muscles? If so, what does that say about their sight and coordination? What about the use of simple machines – the lever, the wheel – in a world with high gravity?

The type of resources a group has will also determine what they can create. A world without much in metals is limited in more than what it uses for building bridges. It will affect many things we take for granted, from cheap eating utensils to canned goods.

Everything about your aliens should link to all the other aspects of their life and world, so the material braids together and nothing stands apart. Consider human hands as an example. Hands are not made to do just one job. We hold hammers with them, but we eat, write, grasp, caress things and test temperatures with our hands as well.

Too many new authors focus on the map-making side of worldbuilding until they can name every city and colony on several worlds. What they don't do, however, is focus on why those settlements exist, how the people survive and how the world rules the way they live.

The Earth is filled with so many cultures we cannot keep track of them all with any ease. We are a fragmented people and this isn't merely a reflection of geography, temperature or religious differences. If you limit your view of culture only to religion, you are missing out on a myriad of ideas to create a fantastic new world and the people who inhabit it.

When creating an alien culture, we sometimes have trouble looking past our own human definitions and insights we've found in studying the people of Earth – but that's all right. You are writing a book for humans to read, which can make it easier to define many different aspects of your aliens. While we can expect there to be things which can't be fully explained, you still have to define what you have in ways the reader will understand.

Culture is everything that ties a group together, it also sets one group apart from other groups. Once you understand the multitude of choices available you can start building something unusual of your own. Or you can make an alien culture which is so oddly human-like that it's unsettling, especially when expectations are not met.

A group of people – or aliens – must have certain things to work together as a unit and this becomes the basis of their culture. These include how they manage their food system, from growing and hunting to distribution and finally to preparation and serving of food. We can often identify the cultural background of a group by the items in their meal, including how they are cooked and presented. There is no reason why your aliens can't also have specific cultural ties to their foods. However, if you are dealing with a space-faring group, the basic food-related aspects of the cultures will have mutated to fit the situation when they are far from home.

How people (human or alien) lived on their home world is going to decide how they live within ships and settlements in other places. If they come from a culture where all the males live in individual huts and the women share a large building, then getting the men to share quarters on a ship might be something so basically against 'nature' for them that they can't do it. This could make it impossible for some alien races to travel with humans unless they can be assured of private quarters. Is eating an intensely private matter? Is bathing a group project? What else can you tweak to change not only how the alien society works, but how it interacts with human groups?

Cultural misunderstandings abound in the real world and can be a source for conflict. Look to such possibilities when you are creating your alien world and populating it. Manipulate your alien creations in ways to purposely create problems for the characters of your books. Conflict is an essential ingredient to stories and it is what keeps the reader turning the page. Every time you find a new level of conflict, you add something more to interest the reader.

Always remember the reader. It's easy to get caught up in the intricate wonder of creating new races and worlds, forgetting that what looks fascinating to the writer and creator will be very boring to the reader who is usually more interested in the characters and the action.

The author needs to know far more about the background than will ever be specifically written about in the book. Knowing this background will help the author be consistent in the work and also present logical options for decision making. It will also give more opportunities to introduce problems. The more an author can see of the world they are creating, then the more opportunities they will see to make things into obstacles. Stories are always about the obstacles the characters overcome, so always be on the lookout for them.

The daily life of aliens

Even if an author works out the basics of what an alien is like, this still doesn't determine what the aliens will act like in any given situation. Having the body is a good first step, but next comes the harder section – the personality and culture. As humans, we act as we do because of our shape: we stand upright, reach with our hands, bow or shake hands in greeting, smile and nod. How does the shape of the aliens affect what they do? How do they greet each other? If we smile and shake hands in some cases, what could the aliens do differently?

When creating aliens, the best thing you can do is ask questions like how and why. Look at every aspect of your creation and decide how it interweaves into the alien's life. Look at the world around you and ask what the aliens would do instead. How do they take their meals? What do they do when they are angry? What is mating and reproduction like?

If you have a group that only comes together for mating, but otherwise is reclusive, then they are not going to develop a civilization. If, however, the females or males stay as a group while the other gender is reclusive, then they can develop civilization. A group has to come together in order to make something larger than its individuals could manage on their own.

Does the alien group have a hierarchy system which involves gender and age? The Romans, for instance, had a very strict system based on their concept of father as the supreme ruler of his group, the *pater familias* or head of the household. This was more than simply the father, though, as such a man might have any number of family members including siblings of both genders under his control and they could do nothing important without his permission. Above the *pater familias* was the patron, the head of a number of clients who paid call on him each day and whom he had the duty to feed each day. Why would he do this? Because the clients gave him prestige when he went out by accompanying him on the streets, which was very important to a Roman. They were also a voting block he could call upon to back what he wanted. A patron could himself be a client of someone else as well, weaving several groups into mutual ties of duty.

Above the patron was the patrician who had the duty of ruling the country in the way the patron ruled clients and the *pater familias* ruled the family. And above him? Jupiter, who is really Jove the Father (you can see the root word 'pater' in the name for father). This was a strong patriarchic (again, note the 'pater') society, though Roman women had far more freedom than did Ancient Greek women.

You do not need a patriarchic society in order to create a strict hierarchy, though. In some animals like elephants, the highest ranking female takes the lead in directing the movement of the rest of the herd, while the larger males keep guard all along the perimeter of the group. If such behaviour carried over into an intelligent race, how would they arrange their cities? How would they adapt to living off-world, and how would they arrange for life on board a ship?

What about communications, from language to written material? Does their world have a viable paper? Or do they write on cloth and perhaps weave the words into the threads?

We can trace the evolution of transportation on our world from walking, to riding, to wagons and to self-powered vehicles. Does the alien world have anything which would be used for a riding creature? Do the majority of their cities sit on huge bodies of water because water transportation developed instead of wheeled transportation? How do they get across wide stretches of land or over mountains?

What does it look like to stand in the middle of an alien city? What do they hear and see? What colours and shapes are their buildings? What do they do there in their daily lives? Where do they get their food and what do the scents tell us about that food? What do the young ones of the society do? How is work handled?

What about schooling? In order for a society to exist, it needs a way to pass down information and cultural heritage from one generation to the next. In the human world, it began with word-of-mouth as people passed information from parent to child. Eventually we developed writing (though it apparently was originally developed only for listing items, for recordkeeping and taxing purposes). Now we have books and computers to store and disseminate information. It would, in fact, be very difficult to wipe out all traces of past history and culture because so much is stored in so many ways and in so many places. Although you have created your aliens for the story, they had a virtual existence before the book. The more you can understand about where they came from, the stronger they will be as characters.

If you go out and walk around your own neighbourhoods you can note all the things that make it unique, from the designs on the buildings to the sounds and scents coming from them. If an alien walked down the street in front of your home, what would it note? These are the kinds of things you want to consider about the aliens and their own lives – then you need to consider how you can change them so they don't seem to mimic human actions. It is difficult to create truly believable aliens without using human terms. We cannot be aliens, so the best we can do is look at our own behaviour and how we are changed by our world and our shape, to see if we can create some twist to make them seem less human.

While this may seem like something which cannot be overcome and will ruin any attempt to create believable aliens, there is another factor to take into account. The reader is human and is going to be looking at the aliens in much the same way as the author does when creating the beings. We all have to see things through the human experience, so if you want your readers to understand the aliens then they have to be able to connect with them. Twisting what is human to make it different for the aliens is important to holding the reader's attention.

Experiment with the aliens. Look at them, look at their world and compare it to the world around you and try to work out a creation which is alien, interesting and readable. It's not an easy thing to create. But if you are going to create aliens, you need to spend considerable time in the pre-writing phase until you find the right combination of factors to create the alien you want for your story.

Aliens can be humans in funny skin or they can be human-like and totally alien in thought-processes and culture. Perhaps they are simply aliens in funny skin. Any one of those can work for the proper story - it's up to the writer to make them work for whatever is needed.

> **What if...**
> This time the humans have found an alien city high up in the mountains of the same world which has the noxious lowlands. What does the city look like? What do the inhabitants look like and how do they greet the visitors?

Naming aliens

This is far harder than it might first seem. The time when you could shove some odd letters together and throw in a couple of apostrophes is mostly gone. The name should be thought out as part of the alien shape and conform to the rules of the alien society. And if you name one alien according to these rules, you must use the same to name others of the same closely-related group.

As humans, we tend to think of names in groups of two or more words. This isn't necessary for aliens. Single names, or names a sentence long, may work in certain circumstances.

Most readers do not stop and sound out the name of a character each time. Instead, they see a word as a tag related to a certain character. Those tags need to be easily recognizable at a glance. If you want to use a naming convention to link a group together, use the western convention of keeping the tag at the end – Kevtar, Delotar and Itar work in the same way as John Jones, Bill Jones and Debbie Jones. It is also best to make the first part of each name different. Characters called Nami, Nani and Nari all look far too much alike to the reader, who is likely to skim over names as they read. The reader's most important link to the character is the name-tag (or in some cases, description tag) you assign to him. Do not give your aliens similar-sounding or -looking names unless your intention really is to confuse the reader.

Another thing you need to consider in naming aliens is the shape of their mouths. This will also come into play later when we discuss language creation. Are there certain sounds which can't be made by your alien?

Are the names which appear in your book actually the names of the alien, or are they the human-translated forms?

If your aliens are dealing with humans, perhaps the name will be translated into human letters and spoken in a way which is more akin to human speech rather than the alien one.

There is also the possibility that aliens could adopt a human name in place of their real one. This might be something to consider if you have an alien society where names are something personal and secret, given only to clan members, or one in which humans can't be bothered to take the care to learn to say alien names properly (or in which they can't because of their mouth shape) and the aliens are tired of having their names mangled.

But the most important factor to take into consideration is how the reader will respond to the name. The prime purpose of the writer is to draw the reader into the story and to do so he has to avoid any little nudge which might throw the reader out of the forward flow of that story.

> **What if...**
>
> What if you had an alien group which was very much like humans, but you want to make them different in behaviour? What changes would you make in their society to make them distinct from humans?

This chapter has covered, in simplistic and very basic ways, how to create aliens and their culture. There is far more to this art than what can be explained in a single chapter, but much of it will be obvious as you work on this type of writing creation. Experiment with ideas for aliens and see where they lead because experimentation, more than following a set of guidelines, will help you find the unique beings for your stories.

In the next chapter we'll look at an aspect of writing which affects both aliens and humans as we explore ideas about language in the future, along with how to make the writing of it intelligible to the readers of today.

6 Language of the Future

- Writing for today's reader
- Creating future words and slang
- Dealing with alien languages
- Move beyond the words

Many people enjoy either creating an entirely new language for an alien race, or sometimes creating a new form of human language for a future civilization. Creating a new level of slang for future teens or gangs can be an exciting prospect. After all, writers work with words, and the idea of creating new words can be a heady experience. There are, however, a few traps in working with constructed languages (sometimes called conlangs) but they can be avoided with some common sense.

Writing for today's reader

When you create either an alien language or a complex slang system for the future, the first thing to remember is that you are *not* writing for those aliens or the people who use the slang. You are writing a book for the readers of today, which means no matter how complex you make your new language, you are still going to have to present most of what the language means in plain old, everyday English (or whatever language you use).

A story in which the reader can't tell what's going on is useless. While a bit of language which isn't understood can add interest and tension to a story, too much of it will lose the reader's interest. Having to read something with a dictionary of some sort in hand, for instance one translating the extensive alien language tracts from the pages, can turn the pleasure of the story into a chore. Make certain that

75

whatever alien language you include provides enough spice to improve the story, but not so much as to overwhelm it.

Language started as a function of cooperation but has become a tool of information and entertainment. As Steven Pinker says in *The Language Instinct*, 'writing is an artificial contraption connecting vision and language.' Because it is unnatural in many ways, authors tend to write made-up words to look good and forget to really sound them out. English, which has borrowed so much from so many other languages, has a number of variables for letter combinations. This makes it an eclectic language when writing new words but it can also be very confusing as some letters can be written to produce different sounds.

George Bernard Shaw had a special dislike for the English alphabet, and pointed out that he could spell fish with the letters 'ghoti' ('gh' as in tough, 'o' as in women, and 'ti' as in nation). With such kinds of possibilities, it is often difficult to create a word that others will understand and pronounce properly. Also, keep in mind how the letters look as well as how they will sound. Using odd letter combinations may not be as clear to others as they are to you.

Creating future words and slang

Language does change over time. We are not speaking the same English spoken at the time Shakespeare wrote his wonderful plays. Some of the terms he used confuse readers of today despite their understanding almost everything else being said. Word meaning and slang have changed over time. We can expect future language to change as much, if not more, especially since we are merging more and more words from foreign languages into everyday speech.

New technology also brings new words with it: Internet, blog, dial-up, broadband, email and dozens of other words would have meant nothing to someone fifty years ago. It is also possible for one generation to have trouble understanding what another generation is saying because of the use of slang and the shift in language. If you have groups which separate themselves from the larger section of humanity, both languages will diverge if there is no regular contact.

So, you can expect there to be changes in language. You can incorporate those changes into your story to help create a feel of the future you want to portray. It can be exciting to start out with the terms and build understanding as quickly as possible and make the meaning of the words obvious through use.

When creating a few new words and terms, look at what changes you've made in your future world. This is where the ripple effect of worldbuilding comes back into play again. If you have created a major new industry or a shift in culture of any sort, there will be a new series of related words springing up around it.

Finding those words can be a wonderful addition to a story. Start out slowly with one or two words at a time and use them in ways so it is relatively easy to tell what they mean. If necessary, and if it can be done in a natural way in a story, have someone translate for a newcomer on the scene. Such a situation might occur when someone first arrives on a new world where the language has adapted to the unique situations found there.

What if...

Aliens have introduced a fast-growing, addictive fungus to humans. It is hallucinogenic and has reduced some areas to nothing more than fungus farms. What terms might spring up for this item? What slang and what words in the alien language would work and how would the alien word translate into English?

Dealing with alien languages

There are rules of English making it something of a 'set in stone' language compared to a few of the others. English has, among things, a fixed subject-verb-object order, this means that 'Dog bites man' and 'man bites dog' mean two different things. But in some languages the verb always comes first, while in others the order isn't as important as the qualities assigned to the words that indicate who or what is performing the action. Imagine a language in which the verb and subject are one word: dog-biting, dog-rests, dog-ran, etc. In a language like this, the different states of the object would be combined into the nouns.

Now consider assigning gender and number to a noun, so you would know if the dog was female and if there was more than one dog without adding other qualifiers.

Playing with things like gender tags, word order and other grammatical rules can help create the feel for an alien language when your character is translating the language into English. Some of the alien grammar rules will be so ingrained that translating the sentence into 'proper' English might be impossible for a native alien speaker.

Other aspects of creating an entirely new alien language present problems for the author. First, you often don't want your aliens to be exact copies of humans, so you need to think of ways to make their language reflect thinking in ways which are not along the same lines as human. One way you can do this is to apply a word in English which would not normally be associated with the object or activity. For instance, if an alien says he is 'heading for bed' that might mean he is going to a small closet where he hangs from his feet. In this case 'bed' has become a synonym for a place of rest and has nothing to do with how humans use the same word.

You might consider whether the language used by your aliens would be influenced by their genetics. In humans, a gene exists in chromosome 7 which is linked to a condition known as specific language impairment. This seems to indicate that language itself has some genetic link. Would aliens have this link at all? Would they, like some people suffering from specific language impairment, have a general problem with grammar which might include misunderstanding tenses, word order and plurals? Would aliens who are less human-like be unable to understand most of the human language?

If your aliens are sufficiently human-like to interact with your people from Earth, then they will have some common ground in thinking and language. Basic terms which translate easily may be as far as the communication goes between the two groups.

You may also consider the use of a 'dead' language as a common ground between groups. Latin continued to be used in communications long after it had stopped being spoken because, as a dead language, it did not fluctuate in meaning. People who did not speak the same languages could still communicate via Latin as an international language because the words did not change over time. What had been written a hundred years before could be understood by someone who spoke German, French or Italian, although the original author did not speak the same language as the reader. This shows how the use of Latin created a form of communication transcending both time and place. People did not need to know multiple languages to communicate with each other through books and letters, they only needed to learn to read and write in Latin. In circumstances like this, if both groups accepted that the word for 'starship' was written as 'stshp', then it wouldn't matter what language they said the word in, so long as they both understood the concept for which those letters stood.

Thinking in these terms, the author might create a trade language, composed of key words from both languages, that provides enough understanding for two sides to deal with each other under fairly friendly terms. Or, if there were multiple alien groups, one might be the middleman and their language would dominate the communications between all groups. This, of course, would bring up the question of how trustworthy such twice-translated communications can be.

Always look for ways that things such as language can create trouble, be misunderstood and add problems to your story. While you are trying to create a viable, working situation for your humans and your aliens, you are also looking for a way in which to create tension in your story.

In C.J. Cherryh's *Hunter of Worlds* the alien languages are wonderfully integrated. In this novel there are four groups learning to deal with each other: humans, Kalliran, Iduve and Amaut. The author does an excellent job of introducing alien words and ideas, so by the end of the book a person usually has no trouble understanding any of the terms.

> **What if...**
>
> When trying to come up with an alien language, the problem may be to find things that are shared and things that are not. Look around your immediate area and consider what you would expect aliens to have (buildings? furniture?) and what they would not (cats? books?). If the aliens could not make the sound of the letter 'B', how would this affect the words of their language and the words they adapted from human language?

Move beyond the words

We tend to think of language as made up of nothing but sounds, yet we often use gestures and facial expressions to modify what we are saying. If you have created an alien race which is significantly different from humans, then coming up with gestures and expressions to help them convey language could be a fascinating and rewarding addition.

Seeing how your aliens communicate might help you to better refine their physical features as well. Cover everything from what is considered polite and friendly to what is rude and obscene. If you have a set group of gestures and expressions, you can relay information in subtle ways. For instance, if an alien always bows his head down to his chest every time he says 'this is the truth' then the one time he doesn't do so when he says those words can be a major clue in your story.

We learn a great deal about other people from their facial expressions. It's one of the reasons online communication is often so filled with misunderstandings as the reader 'hears' things which were not intended, or misses things that were. But facial expressions can also be misunderstood, so when you are dealing with characters who have not been raised in the same culture (human or otherwise) such misunderstandings can be an important part of the story. What if the baring of one's teeth is considered by your aliens to be a sign of unbridled rage verging on an attack, while in the humans it's just smiling?

We also use clothing as a form of communication every day, especially when you think about various uniforms. What about make-up, clothing and accessories as forms of communication? Colours and style might provide clues to moods, impart information about business or family life, or convey any other situation the author cares to work into the story.

Scents might also play a part in communications. We take a lot of scents for granted and don't notice many of them as we move through our daily work, while the animals around us are often far more attuned to them.

Touch? Touch could be an important part of communications in an alien race. How would aliens interact with humans who are often very territorial about 'their space' and touch-phobic in some cases?

What all this means is that if you want to create a truly different alien language, try combining more than words. You might come up with something truly unusual and memorable. However, you cannot let the alien language or your human slang overpower the story you are trying to tell.

What if...

What if you had an alien race which communicated primarily through scents? What might they adapt from human scents and perfumes to communicate things to humans? Humans are rarely as aware of scents as they could be. How would this affect human reaction to scents as well? If humans understood the meaning of scents, would they adapt the same things for themselves?

We have discussed some of the simple concepts of language, but this is – again – a subject that could take entire books to explore. This chapter has tried to introduce you to ideas, helping to point you toward topics you might want to research yourself in more detail.

In the next chapter, we'll discuss the idea of where to place your story based on the needs of the tale you want to tell. Whether a tale on a future Earth, or a story placed light years away, deciding what is best for the story will help you create worlds that work with your plot and your characters.

7 Staying Close to Home

- Placing a story on Earth
- The pitfalls of staying too close to Earth
- The first colonies
- Moving away from Earth

The location for your science fiction is only limited by the story you want to tell. Whether you want to keep it close to Earth in both time and space, or range out into the wider universe, is up to you. Both have their appeal and have avid readers. Chances are that if you write enough science fiction in your life you will write stories based in a variety of places. Making those locations different – alien – is going to be a challenge.

Placing a story on Earth

Let's start at home and work our way outward…

Placing a story on the future Earth is an exciting challenge. In an earlier chapter we talked about how small changes lead to big ones, and when creating a future Earth as your setting you need to apply this method of thinking to your actual worldbuilding. For many people on Earth, life has changed drastically in the last one hundred years and you may predict a future where such change has continued – or alternatively, one in which we reached stagnation or where civilization fell back.

The only thing you can't do is make your Earth of the far future the same as the world of today. Humanity has never remained stagnant and while there have been centuries where little technical progress was made (or so it would seem to us), those days are long past. Humanity might fall back to a darker age, as far as technology is concerned, but we would not stay there. We already know the way forward, and no disaster could erase all that knowledge without destroying all of humanity as well.

If you think people might forget how to read and would no longer be able to access the hoards of knowledge we have deposited in every library and computer cache in the world, consider how humanity has been able to decipher ancient languages like Sumerian cuneiform and Egyptian hieroglyphics without even knowing how the languages were actually spoken. It would be hard to imagine a future with all knowledge lost... but perhaps you can for your book. It is your imagination and work which will make it real.

Designing the Earth of your future depends on whether you believe we are going to keep making progress, reach a plateau and remain there, or if we are going to have a catastrophic fall of civilization and have to rebuild. If the people rebuild on the foundations of the former technology, it doesn't mean what they create will all be exactly the same. For better or worse, technology – and the culture existing around it – will not be exactly the same as it was before.

I'm stressing this because too many new writers paint a veneer over the current world and never look beneath the thin coat of 'change' they've created. Everything has to be examined, from housing to transportation and from food to clothing. Education and religion are both important aspects of the future, no matter what type of future the author imagines. They have always been an important part of human culture. Education is not simply sending children off to school; it is the passing on of cultural heritage and family history, it also includes the simple things like learning how to cook and sew.

If your story is based firmly on Earth, this doesn't mean you will have an easier background to work with. Earth is an intricate world; examining even a small section of it will reveal complexity which, though often overlooked in our everyday life, is crucial to an author who needs to study and use it to create the best story possible.

The pitfalls of staying too close to Earth

Placing a story 'too close to home' can blind the writer to the effect the world itself has on the story. For instance, adding aircars means more than just a change in how the characters travel. Before the age of cars, many small villages grew up in a haphazard way with no straight or wide paths between buildings. If ground transportation is no longer common, then new building developments might well return to a less than logical pattern. Newtown would look quite different from Oldtown. And what happens to the art of giving directions? Does every building have a built-in ID broadcaster, helping anyone in an aircar locate their destination? Are roof-top landing pads common? Have some buildings sprung up in the middle of four-lane highways? How is rubbish collected? What does everything look like?

This is the heart of worldbuilding for a future on Earth. There can be familiar elements that people will recognize in your setting, but how far into the future and what changes you build into your story will dictate how much of the present world you need to change.

The moon, Mars and the satellites of Jupiter or Saturn are all popular colony destinations, but they present a problem for authors. Every year we learn new things about our solar system and sometimes those things can impact the veracity of your work. The changes can come too quickly to make corrections in a work already on the path to publication. Even while I was writing this chapter, a CNN article announced that the solar system's envelope is dented, rather than symmetrical, and this is caused by the magnetic field lying between star systems. Change happens every day, in both small and great ways. No writer can anticipate what will happen next.

We are always learning new things about our solar system and discarding outdated information. This doesn't mean you should avoid a setting within the solar system, but you must be aware of the problems it can entail. It also means you have to be as knowledgeable as you possibly can be about what is already known. While we look back at the *John Carter of Mars* books with nostalgic warmth now, the same will not be true of a story which should be well-researched by current knowledge, but is not. It is unlikely such a story would find a publisher. People who deal in the business of science fiction today are very much aware of what the reading public will accept, and poorly researched material is something that will ruin the chance of a sale, no matter how interesting your plot or how engaging your characters might be.

Exploration stories, without settlements tied to them, are always popular within science fiction, but those placed within the solar system also need special care to make certain everything is up to date. This doesn't mean you can't slip in something unexpected – only that what is already known and real can't be overlooked or ignored.

> **What if...**
>
> What would be some differences between a story placed on the moon in a piece written prior to 1950 and one written today? Here is one hint about something which has drastically changed in our knowledge since then: what is the dark side of the moon?

The first colonies

If you are going create man's first colony away from Earth, chances are you're going to choose a setting within the solar system whether it's the moon, Mars or one of the satellites of Jupiter or Saturn. Being aware of the problems this might create should not derail you from telling the story. You can have an exciting, dramatic tale within range of Earth, as many modern science fiction writers have proven. Building a fictional colony on such a place will be helped by all the real-world research which has already been devoted to the subject.

If you are going to place a story on the moon, there are dozens of books dedicated to the subject, and they'll help you with maps, names, and general information so you will situate the colony on solid ground and show what your characters will see if they look outside.

The near vacuum of the moon is well-suited to some industry work and it is likely to be developed as soon as we have a viable and reasonable way to travel off Earth. Manufacture of some kinds of medical supplies is only one of the many ways colonists might take advantage of the low gravity and near vacuum conditions. Mining for silicon, iron, and other minerals – as well as for oxygen – might all be important in the future.

For Mars, there is one book which is an exceptional resource, not only for the history of the planet's exploration but also its physical shape; this is *A Traveler's Guide to Mars* by William K. Hartmann. This should be a book in the private library of anyone writing about Mars. It also makes a good reference book for creating new worlds as well.

Other planets and satellites are less well-known. So if you are going to spend a lot of time writing about events within the solar system, it would be a good idea to get subscriptions to one or more of the astronomy magazines.

When it comes to writing the story, setting up the backdrop should take into account any kinds of problems you want to create for your colonists or explorers. Subtle manipulation of the setting can help to create additional trouble to add to your storyline as you move along. Adding different levels of danger for your characters can both create a more interesting story, and can also allow for misdirection.

In order to do this properly, you have to think about the type of trouble you want for your story and start building in related weaknesses from the start. It may be an obvious problem, or something which only becomes apparent as the story progresses. Laying the groundwork for this is far easier than adding it in while you are writing the story. These problems can relate to the locations as long as they are obviously not contrary to what is known about the world on which you place the story.

In some cases, writing a story set far enough in the future so the solar system has been changed and adapted by humanity (or aliens) can get you past questions of authenticity if you have a reason to stay 'close to home' in your science fiction story. Or you might come up with one big invention which makes some changes fast and inevitable. Think about how fast our world has changed since the invention of the car, the home computer, and the Internet. A breakthrough in space travel could quickly transform Mars.

Research into areas like chemistry, astronomy, physics also benefit from the low gravity and near vacuum conditions. These are all great starting points for stories or for background to a tale. Probably a colony on the moon would not have a singular focus, but many.

What about a space station? Creating a station with a viable habitat for humans is far easier than terra-forming an entire world, and no more difficult than building a domed colony on a world. A station in orbit around Mars might still make that world a viable industrial site – but you still have to decide what industry to introduce and why it would be important enough to the people of Earth for them to create and maintain the station.

One important use for a space station could be as a transfer point. The larger the ship, the more difficult and costly it is to operate within the gravity well of a world. But locating a station in orbit at the proper Lagrangian points, balanced between the gravitational pull of two large objects, makes it possible for a station to exist in any system with large planetary and satellite bodies. Such a location is desirable because the station doesn't need added power to stay in place.

What if...

What if one hundred years from now there were well-established colonies on the moon and Mars? What would people expect to find there? What would draw people to visit them?

Moving away from Earth

If you are taking your story off Earth, perhaps outside the solar system, there are three basic types of locations you might have to deal with:

1. a spaceship of some sort
2. a colony established by humans
3. an alien-based settlement

You may not have considered that worldbuilding applies when you are planning a spaceship, but if this is a setting in which your characters are going to exist then it must have the same level of detail you would give to a village. The layout of the craft and the look of its sections will play a vital role in your story. If you do not give your ship the depth of detail it needs, your characters will be moving through a grey world – dull and empty for the readers. Some things to consider, besides basic colour schemes, are the use of emblems to designate various sections, the size and shape of quarters, locations of halls, gathering areas, and what plants and art might be used to break up the monotony of the layout. Any ship going long distances shouldn't look like a grey prison cell, unless that's what it is meant to be.

Humans are sense-orientated and creative where any of our senses are concerned. We make art to look at, music to listen to, perfumes to smell, and velvets to touch. Depriving people of sensory input can be a form of torture. This means no matter where humans go, there will be some sort of art created out of the materials at hand. It will be part of the spaceships and colonies wherever humans go. Keep this in mind, because art can create a unique subliminal message in your story and art has been used for propaganda quite often in real life.

If you are building a colony of humans on a new world, you must start with the first basic question: is the world itself human-compatible or not. If not, then what sort of enclosed colony are you going to build? Underground? Domed?

What is the purpose of the colony? No settlement has ever been made without it having a purpose, so this is probably the most important question you can ask yourself. To go through the expense and danger of building a domed colony must mean the rewards are worth the work. A small science station might exist for esoteric reasons, but a colony with thousands of people has to have a reason to be there as well as ways for them to survive.

Where do they get their supplies? Are they able to grow anything at all? How about equipment needed to keep the domes viable living areas? How does the group handle any growth in population? If they are dependent on outside resources, how often do those resources arrive? What happens if the supplies are late?

It might seem unreasonable for a colony to be dependent on outside supplies, and it is likely the settlement would try to supply as much of their own needs as they could. However, consider that every large city on Earth is also nearly completely dependent on outside resources. While this might not be quite as dangerous as being in a colony somewhere worlds away, it is still a situation where delays in supplies could create disaster.

Colonies on terra-formed or terra-compatible worlds would probably not have quite the same limitations. While a terra-formed world would be expensive to create, having a full world to populate would open it up to a more free-flowing population. A terra-compatible world might draw people looking for adventure or people looking for a place to start new. It would be a far more diverse world than the one controlled by the dictates of the limited space and resources.

Much of this depends on who controls immigration to such a place. If you have a story universe filled with settled worlds, such transitions might be fairly common. If you have one with strict controls on movement, then adventurers would be less common.

The two different types of settlements, domed and open, will be faced with one common foe: nature. Both groups will be cautious about local conditions, whether natural disasters come in the form of unstable land or atmospheric conditions.

What if...

What if your character was one of the first to reach a new settlement on an alien world? What would those first few days be like? What if the character came a hundred years later? What would make this settlement still seem alien?

We've looked at a few ideas for writing about stories based on Earth or close to it but there is a very large galaxy out there, filled with possibilities for stories. In the next chapter, we'll look at some of the ways to locate stories away from Earth and the solar system.

8 Space Travel Possibilities

- Home or away
- Exploring the galaxy
- Drive technologies
- Ship types
- Sometimes the story is the journey
- Who wants an adventure?

If the future you imagine has space travel and journeys to new worlds, it will be important to decide how your characters get there and who is likely to go on such an adventure. Stepping away from Earth as the setting for your story opens up a universe full of possibilities, but keeping those possibilities 'real' within the context of your story is very important.

Remember, though, the reader wants adventure. They do not want to be lectured. You can teach the reader a bit about science (or any other subject) but only if you do so carefully and within context of the story. You are not writing a textbook or a travelogue. When researching a story, it is easy to become enamoured of the background material and try to shove in every little detail you have learned. This kind of material can weigh the story down, though, so use what you learn wisely to make a more interesting and exciting story.

Something of key importance in this section is that you recognize the possibilities and limits of space transits, and also understand what these different types of travel will mean to your characters. Consistency is vital or you will alienate your reader!

Home or away

Many science fiction stories are placed on Earth. These tales range from such fascinating work as John Brunner's *Stand on Zanzibar*, which foretells a frightening future for an overpopulated Earth, to post-apocalyptic tales like David Brin's *The Postman* and Larry Niven and Jerry Pournelle's *Lucifer's Hammer* both of which explore the hope of survival despite the fall of civilization. Science fiction tales need never leave Earth and they can be stories of future utopias as well as future hells.

However, when most people consider the science fiction genre, they think about stories based elsewhere, whether on the moon or in some far star system. In some cases, the beings on those far worlds might have no connection to Earth's humanity but other stories are about members of the human race in some faraway place, dealing with things strange, wondrous and dangerous. Where your characters go and what they find is only limited by your imagination – and this imagination of science fiction writers has served to create some of the most fantastic adventure stories set in exotic and alien locations.

How your characters got there is a major important step and one which has to be carefully considered. Any science fiction tale moving away from Earth has to deal with travel of some sort; if it isn't covered convincingly, it can be another of the breaking points where some readers will put a book aside. You do not need to give over pages of story on how the ship's drive engine works, but what is there has to be consistent throughout the book.

Knowing how your characters got to their location (or how they are in the process of getting there) is a major aspect of worldbuilding and will affect everything from who goes on the adventure to whether or not they are on their own.

Exploring the galaxy

Moving away from the solar system and what we know today (and might learn tomorrow) can give your imagination more range to create something unique, if this is what you want to write about. You can set up planetary systems the way you want, create new worlds and envision new challenges. Of course, a lot of this will depend on what type of space travel you want to have as well.

There is still the pesky science you need to consider when creating your new system. You must know the basics of astronomy and physical cosmology if your characters are going to venture out into the stars. Understanding gravitation, atmosphere, tidal waves, weather and all the things which make our world what it is will profoundly influence any world you create, whether the planet is Earth-like or not. Understanding the difference in types of stars and why some are more likely to have planetary bodies than others will help you create a believable setting. Whenever you set out to make a new star system be sure to review the important factors for creating such a place, including how gravity influences both land mass and the physical make-up of any aliens. If you are going out into the stars, make the journey believable.

Adjusting what audience you are aiming at can allow you a little more leeway in your worldbuilding. If you want to draw the hard science group, you must stick to strict 'how we know it works' rules and build your universe based on those rules. However, some types of science fiction, such as space opera, allow authors to adhere less strictly to scientific absolutes (as currently known). So targeting readers of this type of science fiction allows for a more 'what if it worked a different way?' approach, whereas the hard science fiction reader is unlikely to welcome light speed ships or human-like aliens. Of course, this does not mean wonderful stories haven't been written using both styles.

The trick when writing anything of this sort is to be consistent and make the material work within the confines of the story universe. Consistency also allows you to create break points and trouble areas and be able to apply them in ways which will not look haphazard to the reader. Consistency should also carry through to all the science and technology in your story. If you create any sort of device from a ship engine to a weapon to a portable food container, think how the technology works and how it can be linked and carried through to other elements of the story. Remember (again) the ripple effect which has been stressed before: everything affects the rest of the world around it.

Creating this material is more than just making a list of things to add into the story's background; you can use and manipulate any of it to create the trouble you want to occur in your story. This is a very serious aspect of writing because finding problems the characters have to overcome is what draws in the reader to continue with the story. So if the characters are faced with problems outside the main plot, it adds tension to the story.

There is one other important aspect of working with this type of material and this is to be able to fit your characters to the time period in which they live. If there is technology common to your story universe then your characters need to be aware of most of it without noticing and it needs to be a part of their lives. We rarely take special note of the technology running our lives and your characters should act the same way.

> **What if...**
>
> What would a failure of the major power system mean in a domed colony or on a ship? Which systems would fail? What would have automatic backups? What could they have in portable equipment which might help?

Drive technologies

Deciding on how humanity travels from Earth will determine how far and how fast your people will go. Leaving Earth at all requires a considerable amount of force and for this reason it is likely that larger ships will not be planet-based at all. Gravity wells are powerful forces and the amount of thrust needed to break free of them required a larger ship to stay as far out in the gravity well as possible. This means that a behemoth of a ship might come no closer to a planet than a space station where people and supplies can be offloaded into shuttles and transported to planet-side destinations. Such a ship need not be designed to be aerodynamic, either.

So we have a potential path either off your world or all the way to the stars. Now how exactly do we use it to get where you want to go?

The types of engines which have so far been used to reach space are far too inefficient to propel humanity beyond a few exploratory trips to check things out in our own neighbourhoods. Science fiction authors and scientists – who are often visionary by their very choice of profession – have already begun the design work for such craft.

In the next few paragraphs are very quick explanations of some types of engines which can work as the basis of spaceship engines. If any of them sound reasonable for a story, more research will help you to define the parameters of how they might work and help you to make a proper setting in which to employ them.

The Bussard Ramjet, simply explained, would use a magnetic field facing forwards to gather hydrogen from space and funnel it backwards into a reactor where it would be converted into plasma. It would then use the power of the plasma as thrust to move forward. Hydrogen is readily available in space (which is not quite a vacuum), so the ship would always have a fuel source. It is a sub-light engine, but one which can move a ship virtually anywhere and for any length of time.

A ship using solar sails would gather light from stars and use it for propulsion. This might be a good choice for interplanetary travel where solar light is plentiful. The sails would be huge and fragile, however. Such a ship would likely have a system for folding the sails down if they came into a dangerous area. Momentum would still carry the ship forward for some way, but any gravitational pull would also drag it off course.

Fission power is used in nuclear power generators and in the earliest atom bombs. It splits a heavy nucleus into two smaller nuclei which can produce combinations of light nuclei as long as the number of protons and neutrons in the resulting creations equals the number in the original nucleus. Energy is produced because of the difference in mass between the lighter nuclei and the heavier, original nucleus. Mass that is lost is translated into energy. Obviously, fission power is not the best way to harness nuclear power because of the large amount of radioactive waste it generates.

However, it can produce a huge amount of energy from a small pellet of fuel and in the depths of space disposing of such radioactive waste might not seem so difficult.

Fusion power is created when two light nuclei combine to make a heavier nucleus and the process releases energy because the mass is less than that of the two original nuclei. One hope for future power is to combine two hydrogen isotopes to form a helium isotope. Fusion power in many ways is the hope of the future since it combines into something stable, unlike fission which produces three types of radiation.

Fission and fusion power could create faster-than-light speed, depending on how the power is harnessed and what the engine itself is like. Obviously, since nothing like this has been invented yet it would be up to the author to create this in ways best suited their work.

Black holes have been suggested as sources of power for spaceships and other technology. In Larry Niven's *The Hole Man* such a mini-black hole was held in a containment field (which was all alien-designed). More recently, it has been found that power sources can spin outward from a black hole in the form of magnetic fields and chaotic gas. Black holes have often been considered gates to elsewhere, at least if the traveller could somehow survive going through.

Science fiction writers often come up with unique ways to propel ships to their new destinations. One way to get around the 'beyond human knowledge' problem is to have the technical ability come from another source: aliens. Alien jump gates often litter the science fiction universe and alien technology can give humanity a quick, but not quite understood, boost into the stars.

The last fictional way to travel from one place to another is to use a somewhat metaphysical wave of the hands with a sprinkling of quantum mechanics and a belief in *other* places that can be reached with some kind of power or engine which will open a door – and close the door again on the other side. While this probably sounds like something more akin to fantasy, it can still be a viable, far future method of travel for people who want to move outside what might be considered the norm. It allows for odd concepts of time and space and for the idea of multiple universes.

How spaceships are moved will also play into what type of craft they are and how you intend to use them in your story. This is something the writer needs to consider when moving off Earth and away from the solar system. But unless it is vitally important to the plot to know exactly how the ship is powered and through what engines and controls, don't fret over it for too long. This is background work to help the author understand the basics of the world in which he will be writing.

> **What if...**
>
> What if a breakthrough in science made faster-than-light ships possible within the next ten years? Would humanity take up the challenge to go exploring? What if the work required global cooperation of some sort? How long would it take to gain such cooperation?

Ship types

Along with its engine type, the author needs to consider the actual use the ship will have in the story. Carrying passengers? Preparing to seed a new world? How far are they going and how fast will they get there?

If the ship uses cryonics – the freezing of a living creature for future revival – it can be based on known science, albeit one which is still not proven to be reliable where fully grown humans are concerned. The chance of cellular damage to the body because of ice crystals is one problem, along with oxygen deprivation. Current science does not have the adequate resources to revive someone preserved through cryonics, but some people believe nanotechnology may provide the answer.

Robert Heinlein's *The Door into Summer* is probably one of the best known books about cryonic suspension and revival. There are other stories that take the process away from Earth, allowing people onboard ships travelling well below light speed to visit very distant places. Obviously, the people on such ships could not come home again to the world as they knew it when they left: these people are sailing off the edge of the world.

Some sort of stasis which is not cryogenic might also be possible, but this is not within the realm of what humans have figured out at all yet. However, this is science fiction... you can imagine how it will work. Allen Steele's recent *Coyote* series used variations on this, updating a classic science fiction theme into a powerful storyline.

If such a ship was transporting a colony in some sort of controlled sleep, it would take a powerful computer to both find a viable world and make arrangements for its settlement. It might be that the ship's computer begins terraforming a world centuries before the ship begins awakening its passengers.

So a ship using cryogenics is one of two feasible ways to get people to a new world outside our solar system based on what we know and can create using science which is almost possible right now. It would most likely be used with a sub-light speed drive, unless the people were traveling to the far side of the galaxy, where even fast ships might take a long time to reach.

The second type of spaceship which could be used at sub-light speed would be a generation ship. This is essentially a small, self-contained world capable of sustaining life within it over several generations. With the proper power source, such a ship could travel at sub-light speeds and deliver a future generation to a world hundreds of years after leaving Earth.

Such a ship would, of course, have to be entirely self-sufficient. The balance would be incredibly important, and everything from the birth rate to individual food consumption would have to be carefully monitored. The gene pool for the humans – and any animals, of course – would have to be diverse enough to ensure that at the end of several generations those who landed on the new world would still be robust and ready to take on the work of settling a new world.

Generation ship stories often seem to have two themes, and sometimes those themes are interlocked. First, after several generations the people forget there is anything outside the ship, or that they have a destination. Second, and sometimes linked with this theme, is a theme involving a catastrophic accident that damaged the ship, destroying information and possibly crew who had knowledge of how to properly run the ship.

One of the drawbacks to writing a story about a generation ship, however, is the absolute limitations the world places on the storyline. This is a world in miniature, where good and bad can happen and where odd changes in culture can result from small changes on the ship. Interesting plot developments can be imagined on such a journey, including those involving outside forces if you so desire.

The use of spaceships that travel faster than the speed of light takes us beyond anything remotely possible by current scientific knowledge. But such ships are still mainstays of the science fiction world because they present possibilities which take us well beyond what we can do now – and that's what some people see in the future.

We truly have no way of knowing what mankind may invent or come to understand in the future. However, we do have a tendency to 'make real' things we once only imagined. If it can be done, there will be light speed ships (and more) in the future.

Having transportation moving at faster than light speed can open up the galaxy to the science fiction storyteller. It allows characters to visit star systems so far beyond our current range of view that anything can be created there and not risk it being countered by new information, like might happen if your story stays within the solar system.

Moving at light speed is not instantaneous, however. Consider that it takes about 8.4 minutes for light from the sun to reach the Earth. So if you want to move your characters a long distance in a short time, you must move them far *faster* than light speed. Getting them outside the galaxy would take incredible speeds. The distance to the Andromeda galaxy is about 2,300,000 light years (a light year being a measure of distance not time; namely, the distance that light can travel in a year). It takes over two million years for light from the

Andromeda galaxy to reach Earth, so the speed needed to travel so far within a human lifetime would be several magnitudes greater than the speed of light.

No one knows quite what it would be like to travel at the speed of light, of course. Einstein's theories talk a great deal about the differences in ship-time and real-time when ship speeds approach light speed. His work deserves some attention if you are using light speed and near light speed ships in your stories!

Science fiction writers have speculated on the experience for a long time now, and different visions of this type of travel are always appearing in stories. You can imagine your own version, along with your own dangers to go with it.

You might choose to use spaceships in your story as little more than taxi and bus services from one system to another, with most of the action not taking place on the ships themselves. But even so, you still need to know the basics about how the ships work. If you have colonies outside Earth's solar system which your people have travelled to on a fast ship, then you need to know the basics of how fast and how far they travelled. This will affect your story because colonists who can expect help from off-world in a few days will have a far different attitude than people who don't expect help to arrive for months. It will affect their culture, their daily lives and most especially how they view disasters.

Choose what suits your story. Choose something different for a different story, or start building a coherent science fiction universe for a series of stories. Deciding how your people travel, where they are going, and how long it will take to get there is a major part of any science fiction written about anywhere off Earth.

What if...

How would travel on a light speed ship carrying passengers on holiday differ from one transporting colonists? How about a supply ship versus a military craft? What would such a trip be like at sub-light speed within the solar system instead? Don't forget to consider the difficulties of communication!

Sometimes the story is the journey

Sometimes a science fiction story is about the journey to a new world or about travelling from world-to-world (the *Star Trek* Syndrome). Sometimes it is about actually reaching a new world and the journey is only a reminder that the characters are no longer home and aren't just taking off on a quick jaunt to the country for the weekend.

In the first case, where the story is really about the journey, a great deal of detail needs to go into the ship, the crew, and the interaction between these two factors. Emphasis will be on the ship and what happens there. However, if you want to tell a story about life on a new world, you might do your story a disservice by starting too early, or dwelling too long on the journey to reach the world where the real adventure takes place. Readers are not going to be as interested in the carefully calculated logistics of the journey, the planned education meetings for the soon-to-be-abandoned colonists, or much of the other background work you've done to make certain your story is logically feasible within the terms of your created universe.

Who wants an adventure?

One more very important aspect in a story moving people off Earth is to consider who would take such a journey? Much of the answer will depend on how reliable your travel methods are and how long such travel has been in place.

During the first few years when space travel is opened up and going to new worlds, it is going to draw mostly adventurous people who want the thrill of going somewhere new and exotic. Experience tells us these are not usually the best types of people to settle new worlds. They are mavericks and wanderers, the type of people who will create problems when they find themselves settled somewhere.

Colonists have to be a different breed. They have to really want to go, they must be resourceful and willing to work hard. They need to share a vision and must be able to work together with others both for the common good and for the future of their world. Or perhaps their only interest is themselves – they might want the opportunity to start again, with no past problems dragging on their efforts.

Finding groups of people willing to leave the Earth and move somewhere totally unknown might prove difficult. There might be groups of disadvantaged people who would be happy to leave behind their blighted lands and settle on a new world. Groups in inner cities could be forcibly removed if the government so decided – but this might make a world filled with hostile people, not the sort of situation anyone wants to create.

Would there be a lottery for settlements? Sign-up sheets? What would it cost to emigrate to a new world or would the government confiscate everything left behind to pay for the passage and the new land? In an over-populated world, being able to ship thousands of people off to another world might be worth the cost. Allen Steele works this theme well in *Coyote Rising*.

In a story universe with multiple terra-formed or Earth-like worlds, and with faster-than-light ships, moving from world to world might be common and deciding to move to a new colony might not be viewed any differently than we view moving to a foreign land. However, once the colonies are established, the reasons to go there might change.

Every new colony would require professionals of one sort or another. While in ancient days it may have been enough for a group of people to band together and set off in search of a new land, people who grew up with modern health care and indoor plumbing are not going to be happy about the idea of roughing it.

If the colonies are not so far away and people can return, professionals might be hired to work in the colonies for a given amount of time. But if the people of the colony are never going to come home, there could be a shortage of professional help to go with them. They might have to train their own doctors, construction professionals, scientists and other vital roles. This training might be something which happens via computer during the journey itself. Multiple people would have to take up the study to make certain there was at least someone who did well. Depending on just one person for an important job would be dangerous, or perhaps suicidal!

Of course, if this is a trip from which no one returns, there will need to be crew for the ship unless it is a computer-controlled ship of some kind. Perhaps the crew is trained from the group of colonists. This would mean leaving Earth could not be a sudden decision to pack up and go as the preparation for such a journey might take years.

Humanity will always have its share of adventurers who want to leap out into the unknown to see what is out there. They're the people of legend – Jason, Columbus and Magellan. However, while they may get something named after them, they are rarely the people who settle in and do the arduous work it takes to make a colony grow. Such steady, hard-working people are heroes, and their stories can be every bit as exciting as Magellan's tale – but that is a different type of story. Not all humans would have the same motivations for taking to space and heading for new worlds.

What if...

What if explorers found a world which was an Earth-like paradise, and could easily support humans from the first day of discovery? Who would go? Would there be any limitations on what they could do? What difference would it make if the world could be reached in weeks, as opposed to the trip being a one-way transit? Would laws be made to keep this world pristine? What kinds of problems would such a world create, both physically and politically?

In this chapter we have looked at some of the possibilities a science fiction writer faces when moving the story away from Earth and beyond the solar system. Fitting the ship to the needs of the story is important, but so is fitting the types of people to the story you want to tell.

In chapter nine, we will look at the government of the future, especially where it might pertain to people living worlds apart from one another. Who is going to have control? What are the options available?

9 Who is In Charge Here?

- The future rule
- United we stand?
- Alone or with others
- How communications influence government

This chapter will explore some of the possibilities for government in the future. We tend to see the future as a mirror of where we are now – our values, our beliefs, and our current governmental structures. But where you set your story and how fast people can travel will have a huge effect on the form – or forms – of future government. Examine the different possibilities and see if the setting for your story might be an opportunity to step outside the usual fare and try something a bit different.

The future rule

Deciding on how your future is run obviously adds levels of detail and trouble to any story. Whether it is a cyberpunk corporation or a benevolent religious rule, there are bound to be problems associated with the choice. There is also always the threat of rebellion because, no matter what the rule, others will not be happy with it.

There is a far more important aspect of government to consider than naming who happens to be at the top of the pyramid. The people in charge not only make the laws, but they also give power to certain people to enforce the laws. Whether the imperial guards or the local police are in charge, these people receive their power from the ones who control the government. This controls the dynamics of a community. If the local policing force is made up of people who have lived and worked in the community all their lives, there is a sense of trust built into the system (though it can be lost). By contrast, if the policing force is made up of outsiders sent into the area and controlled by an administration which is located elsewhere, there might be a feeling of distrust, along with a belief that these people don't understand local needs.

There are many stories about a future Earth under a single government, or a future Earth in anarchy with dozens of little holdings each fighting their neighbours for survival. Dystopias outweigh the utopias in the fiction world. We seem to have always been pessimistic about the future.

Problems make for better stories, so a government opposed to the people it is ruling, or a government losing power and control, will add problems to a story even if they are only handled in the background. Several scenarios like this can work. For instance, if your characters are in trouble and looking for help, a situation where you have already hinted about the lack of policing or military patrols can provide lots of room for expansion in the story.

Below are sections setting out certain types of rule, giving an idea of the diversity available. It is also possible to combine some of these sections – or you might come up with something entirely outside the norm.

Royal lines

Many writers are fascinated with the idea of having royalty in charge. There are several forms this can take.

A monarchy is any rule which is hereditary and life-long. Many countries have been ruled by monarchs from ancient to modern times. This type of rule is vulnerable to abuse by individuals but is also generally stable over long periods. An absolute monarchy is a kingdom where the king or queen has complete power over the people. This might work on a limited scale, but it would be hard for a single person to enforce his or her control over multiple worlds. Under a constitutional monarchy, the ruler is somewhat limited by the rules of a constitution. This gives everyone who lives under the monarch some understanding of what to expect and what can be done.

A government by aristocracy is one ruled by the wealthy or by a hereditary ruling class. This one would work if a group of powerful business leaders formed a government and kept the control within their hands.

In an empire the overall ruler controls several territories, many of them with their own rulers, who answer to him. An emperor must have more than one kingdom under his rule. A section of an empire might be a principality, which is ruled by a prince rather than by a king, thus limiting his powers.

In a diarchy, also called a duumvirate, the government is divided between two equally powerful rulers. This can plainly lead to all kinds of conflicts if the two do not see eye-to-eye on matters. A triumvirate, which was used in the Roman Republic, is a rule by three persons.

Feudalism is associated with aristocracy. In this case, the individual feudal lord is usually awarded property by someone above him (often the crown or monarch), but which he owes them certain taxes on. In turn, the people on the property (his vassals) owe him produce from their lands and sometimes their labour as well, which in part supports him and in part is passed up the line as taxes to the crown. Such a lord usually owes military duty to those above him as well.

A rule by women is generally called a matriarchy, but this is also a reference to any rule in which the control of power passes through the female line. Before the invention of DNA testing, the only certainty pertaining to a child's heritage was through the mother, since any male could have been the father. Because of this, in a matriarchy a queen's only child who was a son might become king, but after him the rule would pass to a relative who was descended from the closest female relative to the former queen.

Patriarchy is the opposite of matriarchy, and in this system both the rule and power rests with males or descends through male line.

Regency is the rule by someone who is not directly in line for the throne, but who holds control either during the minority of the upcoming ruler, or during a time when the ruler is incapacitated in some way.

If you are going to use nobility, then make a list of the ranks and stick to it. You do not need to follow historical lists unless you want to. A simple list might go something like this, from highest rank to lowest:

- Emperor
- King
- Prince
- Duke
- Marquis
- Count
- Earl
- Baron
- Squire

There are many other types of nobility you might want to use, including systems common to certain countries – which might be a clue tying your future back to a specific place. Or, if you are creating an alien royal line, you might come up with terms all your own, though this list can help you translate various ranks.

Religious rule

Religious rule comes in several forms, sometimes dictated by the religion itself. A caliphate, for instance, is a government made up by Islamic civil and religious leaders. In a hagiocracy the government is controlled by a group of people who are believed to be holy, while in a hierocracy the rule is held by the religious clergy. A thearchy is any government based on divine sovereignty, which has been used by many monarchs. A theocracy, on the other hand, is a government directly by religious officials who believe they have divine authority.

Military rule

Despotism is a government in which a single ruler exercises absolute power. The ruler usually comes from a military background, but he might also have a religious or popular backing for his powers. A dictatorship is a form of absolute power but a military dictatorship can be either a single person or a few who are in control.

Totalitarianism is often associated with a despotic ruler. In this case, the ruler has total control over those whom they rule. Tyranny, where the government by a single authority is absolute, is also often associated with despotism especially when the ruler is harsh.

A stratocracy is the term for any government by the military, while a timocracy is a government based on military glory or on a requisite ownership of property. The two requirements for timocracy can be combined where only those who have served in the military are allowed to own property.

Government by the people

A civil government is any government where the laws are made by the people, or by those whom the people have elected to office. One term for this a commonwealth, in which the authority ultimately lies with the people.

A coalition government is when people from two opposing political parties join forces to form a governing majority, but these are often temporary. A collective, on the other hand, is a government run equally by all the members.

While we tend to think of a constitutional government as an elected one, it can also be used in combination with a royal government, such as in a constitutional monarchy which was described above. Who writes the constitution and for what purposes of control will, of course, impact who rules and how they rule.

Democracy is a government by majority rule and is controlled by free elections of the representatives. Who can vote in such an election has a determining factor in the extent to which the term 'majority rule' can truly be applied.

In the parliamentary system, a group of people are elected to the legislature and they in turn elect an executive, such as a prime minister, from among their own members. This is the type of ruling system where a coalition government might hold together for long enough to get someone elected to the executive position, especially if there is no clear majority of one of the parties within the legislature.

Any government in which the power is vested in representatives elected by the citizens is a republic, and any state that is free from outside authority is said to be sovereign. So, a sovereign republic state is one in which the citizens elect the officials and which has no governing body higher than those which they have elected.

Other choices

Some of the types of rule set out above can either stand alone or be used in combination with a different type of rule. For instance, a despotic ruler could be military, religious or royal in nature.

Anarchy is the complete absence of government control. This means there can be no laws to be enforced. It also means there can be no government services, which can include anything from fire departments to garbage collection.

One form of diarchy (which refers to a dual rule) is when a colonial government shares the power to rule with native ministers. This might be an interesting government for shared human and alien rulers who don't quite understand each other. There is no reason why the humans have to be the 'colonial' force, either.

A fascist government is one in which there is a totalitarian, oppressive and one-part national rule which often involves a dictator and which sometimes emphasizes a certain aspect, such as military, national or racist symbols.

Communism is a theory in which all property is held in common and ownership assigned to the state or the community. It is meant to be a classless society, in which there can be no rich and poor since everyone has equal shares in the community. It is linked with socialism, in which both production and distribution of goods are controlled by the community or the state.

In a federal government, the individual units surrender their sovereignty to a central authority, although they still retain some local powers. The opposite of this is a unitary government in which power is held by single central source, with local governments being used only to administer and enforce the laws.

A rule in which the elders have control over the people is a gerontocracy, usually in the form of a council. In a meritocracy, the rule is by an elite group of people who win their posts based on skill or intellectual achievement. Mob rule, or government by the masses, is known as ochlocracy while an oligarchy is government by a small group of privileged individuals. A plutocracy is a form of oligarchy where government is in the hands of the wealthy members of the society. A technocracy is when the government is ruled by experts and technicians – which seems like a very interesting idea for a science fiction story! While the term welfare state is often used disparagingly these days, it really only means a system in which the government is responsible for the well-being of the citizens.

What if...

In the first few years of a new colony on a far world, what sort of government would the people likely choose? Would it be based on what they left behind, or would they look for something different? If the colony started out with serious problems, what difference would this make to the government? Equally important, how would these experiences change the people in that colony? Would they feel stimulated or stifled? Would they be happy or outraged? Is their pride wounded by the situation, or are they proud about how their state worked through the difficulties?

United we stand?

An important first consideration for a government choice is whether or not the people of your story are united into a single government. This could be a single government on Earth or a government which has some sort of influence over various worlds. Or you may set up a number of different types of rule spread through the colonies on distant worlds. After all, it's not as though Earth has ever been under one type of political system. It is likely various types of government would be tried in different areas – not to mention coming up with systems for alien societies.

A question that will help you to define both the type of government and the relationship of the settlers with the rest of the humanity is 'why have they moved away from Earth?' One of the usual causes for immigration is over-population. If there are viable places to settle away from Earth, some people may opt to try their hand taming nature on another world. Some may be given incentives to take up settlement on a new world, perhaps with an option to come back to Earth after they've done a certain amount of work.

War could send refugees to other worlds if they were given the chance to immigrate. War always creates large numbers of refugees who soon realize they have little chance of ever returning home and now find no one else is very interested in taking them in. If such a group could opt to colonize another world, it would give the new settlement a definite ethnic culture.

Natural disaster might also prompt groups to leave en masse and settle somewhere else. Much of this would depend on what sort of worlds were available. Some people might chance going to Mars since it is relatively close and they would have a chance to get back to Earth. This would be especially so after settlements there started to become commonplace and if any sort of terra-forming created a reasonably comfortable lifestyle.

Moving farther away, especially to worlds from where there would be no coming back, might be harder to sell to prospective colonists. If the people would have to live in domes, they might not be so thrilled about the idea of going there –unless things were so much worse at home, or if there were some incredible payback for going.

Some groups could be forced to leave, causing hostility between the home world and the new one. If these were prisoners, armed guards would be required on the trip. The prisoners would probably be stranded on the new world with little hope of any outside contact for as much as a generation or more. Why would a government go to the expense of doing something like this? If the world had something they wanted, and they promised the prisoners repatriation for doing a certain amount of work on the colony, might the arrangement work better?

Alone or with others

When humans move out into space, they are probably going to settle in different places and live under different rules. Don't be afraid to play with the different parameters for governments and see if you can't come up with something which might stretch the boundaries a bit. However, as with everything, consider how the government will affect the lives of your characters and how day-to-day jobs are done. Unless you are specifically writing about a government that is not working, you need to pay special attention to this area. Who is in charge can have a huge impact on your story.

If you are creating a science fiction universe in which there are other intelligent beings, then how they interact with humans and with each other becomes a major focus of the story. An important part of this interaction is the understanding of each other's laws and how they apply to each group. In the days of the Roman Empire, it was valuable to be able to claim Roman citizenship rather than local citizenship because the Roman laws were relatively lighter and sometimes more humane.

So who has the upper hand in handling the aftermath of an incident involving aliens and humans? We use laws to regulate everything from right of way on the roads to taxes – not to mention who has the right to call up the military. While it is likely each group will have their own laws in their own places, as it is on Earth now, there may be times when they share space or cross paths. If this is a common occurrence, then there will be protocols and rules to avoid any unnecessary trouble between the various groups. That, of course, means it might not work. There can be obvious prejudice on one side or the other – or problems can arise from a simple misunderstanding over culture.

> **What if...**
>
> Mankind has moved off Earth in the stars and founded several colonies. While there isn't always complete agreement on how some of the colonies should be run, there is no major trouble. However, aliens have appeared. The aliens have superior ships and new technology and are willing to share with anyone who joins their federation. Are there types of colonies that might be tempted? How would the governmental power on Earth react if the colonists wanted to join the alien federation?

How communications influence government

One the biggest problems surrounding a far-flung empire or any collection of colonies and settlements, no matter what their governmental system, is the limitation of communications. If there is a central government, then there has to be a way to communicate with and control the outlying settlements, and the farther away the settlements are, the less control the main government can have. Communications are limited by the fastest available transport. In most cases on Earth, communications are now virtually instantaneous because we use radio waves and satellites to relay messages. Not long ago, however, the fastest form of communication was by horseback, mail carriage and sailing ship. Communications in your story may well be limited to the speed of your spaceships, so if you do not have travel significantly faster than light speed then some settlements could be out of the communication loop for years.

The longer it takes for communications to reach far settlements, the less dependent those settlements will be on the central government for guidance, and the less likely it is that the distant government will be attuned to their special needs. Such distant relationships can still be useful, though. If the settlement relies on supplies from home to help them through as they fight to establish themselves on the new world, they will stay tied to the government. Or perhaps the government protects them with a military presence and helps keep others from raiding what would be a vulnerable settlement. Or perhaps, on the other hand, the government keeps an iron-fisted control on all its settlements but is resented by those who have moved so far away from the government's location specifically hoping to get out from under its control.

Whatever the situation, the limits of communication and distance will dictate how much control an off-world government will have on a settlement in space. Those limits also mean that knowledge of what is happening at home will take a long time to reach the settlement: news of disasters, elections, changes in policy, wars... all of these will be slow in arriving. A complete change in government might come long after the deed is done, leaving a loyal settlement in a bad position with the new government though they may not know it for a while.

With the idea of communications in mind, it becomes clear that local settlements are going to be caught up in local current trends whether in government, clothing or entertainment. The local settlements will, therefore, tend to be homogenous in look and sound. Changes in culture will ripple through them and news might spread as quickly by word-of-mouth as by official sources.

Local settlements will also likely be more crowded and possibly reactionary when it comes to perceived and real trouble. The closer a particular group is to the seat of government, the more protesters there will be. There are lots of areas for trouble if you are writing about such a settlement.

Places which are farther away are going to be have more of a frontier feel and could face troubles that those closer to the core of civilization would not, such as first contact with aliens. They will seem backward compared to the closer colonies and tend to be old-fashioned (in whatever way the term might mean in the future).

The more dangerous the world is, the stricter the rules will likely be as well. This is for the protection of everyone because if one person is careless on a dangerous world that would put many others in danger as well.

Such faraway settlements are excellent for setting up something unusual, like the first encounter with aliens, because there are limited resources to call on and the locals have to rely entirely on their own good sense. A settlement of this type is also good a place to try out one of the more esoteric government systems as limited outside contact gives more local control. They are also great places for disasters to occur. Such places, far from the mainline of communications, can allow you to have both high-tech and the feel of the wild, untamed frontier at the same time.

Consider different settings when you look at what you want to write for your story. Spaceships and domed colonies are more vulnerable in times of trouble, while an open settlement gives you a wider variety of settings to work with.

If you are writing a story about a new colony and it has been settled for some time, write a little history of the place even if you don't intend to use it in the story. The first colonists will have faced different challenges than those who come a generation or two later, but there will almost certainly be some pieces of the earlier history reflected in their later culture. Every country and every city in the world is built on the history of what came before, and the same will be true for settlements located on other worlds.

What if...

The assassination of an important political figure occurs on a far colony out on the fringe of Earth-controlled space. It takes nearly three weeks for the first word of what happened to reach Earth, and many months before the news has spread to all areas of the colonies. How does this slow-down in communications affect how the news is received and what is done afterwards?

Choosing the right form of government for a science fiction story can mean experimentation, odd combinations and, if there are aliens involved, thinking beyond the usual human-related parameters. As with everything else, the choice should provide more interest for the story. It should not be something haphazardly thrown into the plot as an afterthought.

In the next chapter, we'll discuss the problem of clichés in science fiction and how to recognize and avoid them – and how to change a cliché into something uniquely your own.

10 It's All Been Done Before

- The challenge of writing something new
- Clichés and mainstays of science fiction
- Time travel stories
- Bug-eyed monsters and invasion Earth
- Relying too much on media science fiction

As their story begins to take shape, writers of all genres find themselves facing the idea of originality. They may have been led to believe certain aspects of science fiction are clichés when they are actually the bedrock on which some types of science fiction are written.

In this chapter, we'll look at some of the ways to use some common themes in science fiction while still making them uniquely your own.

The challenge of writing something new

All writers face the challenge of making something unique and it seems that the fear of not exploring new boundaries is especially strong in the science fiction community. After a short time, however, many writers come to what seems to be a troubling conclusion, fearing that 'It's all been done before'. This creates a situation where many newer writers become upset because they can't find trend-breaking new inspiration. As a result, they give up the idea of writing because they feel they'll only be covering old ground.

It is important to look at those writers who have ventured out into new paths. Truly new, ground-breaking story ideas are rare and they almost always come from writers who have been working in the field for long enough to have a feel for the edges where others might not have ventured. They have often written many other books and stories first, learning to entertain their readers, only gradually moving toward that step beyond what had been the norm. Such feats are seldom made with a single big leap in a writer's first book. This doesn't mean you should give up on the idea of finding a unique idea, but don't avoid writing other stories because doing so will help you hone your skills as a science fiction storyteller.

So whether your interest is in the hard science stories or the soft science stories, find whatever story ideas appeal to you and then write them. It doesn't matter if your story is about the first settlement on Mars and you know there have been dozens of those stories told already. This is *your* story. You will tell a story which is uniquely your own, no matter what elements may have been used before.

What might be a cliché in the hands of one writer can be a distinctive new look at a subject by someone else. The trick is in telling your own story, not only from your perspective but also by considering what you have read in the past and deciding what you would do differently.

Clichés and mainstays of science fiction

If you frequent the Internet looking for materials about writing science fiction, chances are you have come across lists by people telling you to avoid one cliché or another in your writing. Some of these lists are so extensive it would be difficult to find anything in the realm of science fiction you could write about without crossing over one such list's 'don't write this' lines.

There are two problems with such lists. The first is that they should usually be called 'What I'm tired of reading about' rather than saying they're lists of clichés as quite often they are nothing more than a single reader's dislikes and are unrelated to the market as a whole. The second problem is that sometimes they list things as clichés when they are not. A cliché is not time travel, FTL (faster than light) ships, aliens who look human, or anything else that you typically find in science fiction books – these are only elements in stories, a cliché is how you use those elements, including the characters. If you look for twists and new ideas, you will avoid clichés.

If you complied with one such list I came across on the Internet, you would not be able to write a story about androids, faster-than-light ships, anything with a young hero, or any story that involved clones. What this list represented was someone who did not like the *Star Wars* influence. Does this mean *Do Androids Dream of Electric Sheep?* by Philip K. Dick is a cliché? Of course not. How about Orson Scott Card's popular *Ender* stories? No, those stories are not clichés either. In both these examples, the authors took something common to science fiction (android, young hero) and created stories uniquely their own.

When authors copy an idea, character, setting or any combination of those items to create material which is essentially a clone of some earlier, popular work the later works become clichés. This is because the author is not looking for a unique twist to make the material his or her own. If an author creates stock characters who look as though they stepped out of the latest science fiction series, and uses story elements without working them into their worldbuilding, then their story will become filled with clichés.

But avoiding clichés is remarkably simple: never add any element to a story without looking at how it fits within the framework of your story and how you can twist it a little to reflect your own unique approach to the subject. If you are inspired by some other work, look at what you liked in it and find ways to make the characters, setting and technology into something new. Every little twist you make in a story adds to the others, building up into something which has never been written before. Every author has their own story to tell. As long as you listen to your inner voice and look for ways to add, change and twist elements, you'll come up with a story reflecting your own imagination and not a remake of something you've read before.

> **What if...**
>
> All writers are inspired by other books but it takes forethought and practice to use inspiration to create your own work. For this exercise, consider your favourite science fiction story character. What could you do to make such a character of your own, without mimicking the original story?

Time travel stories

One type of story that can too easily fall into a cliché is the time travel story. Too often, writers try to use this type of science fiction to push a personal political agenda ('If my hero had won, things would have been different!') which only works if the author is not heavy-handed in their approach. Since this is also a plot device used in fantasy novels, for instance where someone like King Arthur time-travels into the future, it is a type of story which often draws the ridicule of hard-core science fiction fans. But time travel stories remain popular and there are many well-told tales. As long as the author remembers to keep the ripple effect in mind, they can create a fascinating 'what if' story in which some large or small change in the past leads to a larger change in the future.

Time travel stories have been popular in science fiction for as long as it has existed. We can start, of course, with H.G. Wells' *Time Machine*, a story which would be considered steampunk in today's market. Although it was not the very first time travel story written, it does mark the start of what is clearly defined as the science fiction age. Our fascination with history, and how things might have been changed by a small nudge one way or another, has given us everything from Mark Twain's *A Connecticut Yankee in King Arthur's Court* to Robert Heinlein's *By His Bootstraps* and on to *Doomsday Book* by Connie Willis. Time travel stories have entered the realm of mainstream fiction as well, the most famous being *Slaughterhouse-Five* by Kurt Vonnegut.

However, one pitfall of writing time travel science fiction is not doing sufficient research on the time period that you want your characters to visit. This is also important if you are writing a story in which your characters go to the future, rather than the past. In the case of a future-based story, the research becomes worldbuilding. If the plan is for your characters to have gone on the time journey by accident, not understanding what was going on, you still need to make the details as accurate as they possibly can be within the framework of our current knowledge.

Another consideration is where and when your characters turn up in their travels. While research is easier when dealing with well-known time periods and people, a story based in a lesser known area might allow a new slant – and this is another way to avoid writing something filled with clichés.

Do the time travellers who head into the past change something and thereby affect the future? If you are not really comfortable with the idea of everything unravelling and settling into a new pattern, perhaps you could turn to the idea of an alternate Earth for the results. In an idea born of quantum mechanics, Hugh Everett III suggested that when measuring a quantum phenomenon which could go either right or left, the universe splits between the two choices creating an entirely new universe each time. This, of course, was considered in the realm of science fiction and it does provide an interesting approach when creating an alternate history fiction.

Or you might consider using a conjecture by Yakir Aharonov, who combined quantum theory and the theory of general relativity to create a hypothesis for a time machine. Using Einstein's idea that an expanding sphere with weakening gravity would also speed up time, Aharonov suggested someone in such a sphere might be able to 'tunnel' to the future.

How you make your time travel work is entirely up to you. Time travel stories need not be a cliché if the author is willing to carefully map out both what is real history and what you want to change.

> **What if...**
>
> What if you set a time travel story in a little known section of the Amazonian jungles of South America a hundred years ago? What could such a story accomplish and could anything happen there which would have an effect on the future?

Bug-eyed monsters and invasion Earth

Back in the fifties, at the height of the Red Scare, cheaply made B-movies depicted the horrors of alien invasion and the fall of western civilization. These movies played on the fear of the Soviets invading and destroying civilization as we knew it, and also on the heightened state of distrust spreading throughout the world. This influence also appeared in the pulp fiction books and comics of the age. It was a style of story which pretty much lived and died in the 1950s though some aspects of the 'you can't trust them' (whomever that might be) still lingers, especially in the movie world.

A belief that everything that isn't like us is evil has fallen by the wayside in literature, however, and much of the alien-related science fiction written these days now delves into appreciating the wonders of what makes the aliens different, both physically and culturally. This doesn't mean aliens are all good guys in the newer science fiction tales. Wars are still fought, but the books rarely deal with cases of unreasoning hatred.

This is the key to keeping such a story from becoming a cliché. If your humans are faced with aliens they don't understand, and who don't understand them, the author still needs to know what is going on. It is not enough to throw ugly, bug-eyed monsters into a spaceship and have them attack Earth for no reason. Understanding the 'monsters' and what they are doing will play into the story and add subtlety to it, giving your readers more than they expected.

Relying too much on media science fiction

As mentioned in the first chapter, many science fiction fans, both readers and writers, come to the genre through the aid of the visual media which include movies, television and games. Most are amazed at how different and more diverse they find the written science fiction medium. This is because, in many ways, the visual arts are limited, having to rely on colour and movement to keep the attention of the viewer.

As a result, science fiction movies tend to have overwhelming special effects but lack character depth and development since it is hard to portray introspection. People who come to the written science fiction genre are often surprised (and sometimes dismayed) to learn it isn't all exploding ships and ugly aliens.

It sometimes seems as though the movies get away with the sort of weak plots and huge plot holes which would quickly get a novel rejected from a publisher's slush pile. This also creates a problem for new writers who are not as familiar with the standards for written science fiction.

So if you want to write science fiction, then you must *read* science fiction and not rely entirely on the visual versions as a guide.

Movies, television shows and games can provide inspiration, though. Inspiration comes from many places and watching a thrilling show can help feed your imagination and start it moving toward something that is uniquely your own.

What if...

What if you wanted to tell a story about an alien invasion? What logical reason could you have for the aliens picking this world to invade? What might they want and would there be a way for humans to work with them?

Avoiding clichés in writing science fiction does not mean completely avoiding the mainstays of science fiction like alien battles, FTL ships, robots and young heroes. But it does mean that every element added into the story has to be examined and the author has to find his own interpretation and twist. Every change which moves the story elements away from something commonplace helps to add up to overall originality.

The next chapter, which focuses on character creation, will continue to spotlight the idea of twisting common ideas into making something unique for your story.

11 Creating the Characters of Tomorrow

- Which comes first, plot or characters?
- The four types of characters
- Creating heroes
- Creating villains
- Special problems with protagonists and antagonists
- Secondary characters
- Other characters
- Working with alien characters
- Using archetypes
- Soldier, baker, technoplasma light maker

The heart of all stories is the characters and how the reader reacts to them. This is as true in science fiction, where a character might be an alien blob, as it is in a romance novel. How the author presents the characters and connects them to the reader is as important an aspect of the story as all the worldbuilding and plotting.

Which comes first, plot or characters?

There is no special order in which you have to create your story's pieces to make certain they work properly. Many people are character-driven writers: they see the characters first in their minds and then imagine the situation in which those characters find themselves. Others see the situation first, then people it with appropriate characters. As long as all aspects of the story are given the attention they require, the reader will not be able to tell the difference.

Creating characters that the readers identify with and want to read more about can be daunting. Every character, good and bad, represents aspects of ourselves, so look for both sides of human nature in yourself and in the people you know. Characters in books are often exaggerated in some respects and represent the pure embodiment of their type. The hero might be better than real life, though he still has a few flaws, and the villain could be someone whose unrelenting pursuit of what he wants is tempered only by the true love he feels for someone else. In real life, both representations would seem shallow, but with a book it is important to stress certain aspects, though not so much that the character becomes a caricature.

The most difficult aspect of character creation is using mere words to create a character who lives in the author's mind. It is difficult to translate exactly from the brain into to words, which makes it almost impossible to create characters that all readers will enjoy and understand as well as the author does. The author has special insight and knows the thoughts and personality of the character long before the character is transcribed to paper.

In order for the reader to grasp the depth of a character, the author has to reveal the parts that aren't obvious through that character's words and actions. These last two things translate into personality. Sometimes authors try to depend too much on the words part and don't pay enough attention to the actions. Actions can betray emotions the character is not saying out loud such as suppressed rage, fear and indecision.

What if...

Your character has met with an alien and, while speaking as though everything is fine, he really fears and mistrusts the other creature. How could you show the dichotomy of his feelings through his actions?

The four types of characters

There are essentially four types of characters in stories. The two most important types are the protagonists (heroes) and the antagonists (villains). These are the people you will spend the most time creating and defining. What they do, and why they do it, is as essential to your story as all the work you can do on the science and worldbuilding. If a character's actions do not ring true, you will not hold the interest of the reader, no matter how detailed the rest of the work is or how unique the story idea or world you have created. Readers connect with characters in the story and this is what usually draws them onward through the plot. They want to know what the character will do next.

Creating characters to fit into your science fiction universe is a special challenge. People are influenced by their surroundings, and while we can expect humans to remain much the same (because we have over several thousand years already), adding new dimensions to their world can mean the focus of the characters changes as well.

Integrating characters convincingly into a future world means looking at their world and seeing in what ways it is different from the world of today. One way to get an idea of how those changes might affect your characters is to consider how different our world is from that of one hundred or two hundred years ago. For instance, what we do for work and entertainment is far different from what our great-grandparents did. This is especially so if you are dealing with a post-apocalyptic world or a settlement on a new planet, as looking to the past may give you a special insight into daily life in a similar situation.

Creating heroes

The protagonist, or hero, is usually the main character of a story, though in some cases the main character may be someone close to the hero instead (Dr Watson tells the story of Holmes, although Sherlock Holmes is clearly the protagonist and hero of the stories).

Science fiction is filled with notable characters: from the larger than life characters of Valentine Michael Smith and Paul Atreides, to the unlikely hero of Miles Vorkosigan and the daring Ky Vatta. Unique and wonderful heroes populate the stories and the reader connects with and stays with them throughout, for good or bad. There are born heroes, reluctant heroes and anti-heroes – those people who are darker in nature, but still end up doing the right thing even if it isn't always for the right reasons. A hero has to be a fully-faceted character. Someone who is 'larger than life' only works if the reader can believe such a person really exists. To create the best characters, the author has to be able to blend together all the aspects of a personality, which means both the good and the bad. Creating weaknesses in a character will make him more human and give him added problems, which can help create a more interesting story.

How you set about defining your characters is something you have to figure out for yourself. What works for some people will not work for others. Many authors create detailed character sheets, which can list everything from physical descriptions to family background, schooling and political affiliations. While these can be helpful in defining a character's background they can also become too much of a fill-in-the-blanks exercise, leaving the character far more two-dimensional than if the author allowed some aspects to grow via the story. We are all more than any list we could make to define ourselves, but sometimes authors never look beyond such a list to see what isn't there.

How can you make a fully-fledged character that is ready to fly when he hits the pages? Try to think like the character instead of like the author. Sometimes it's hard to dismiss the 'What would I do?' in favour of 'What would this particular character, with her background, do?' instead. Author Holly Lisle sometimes has her characters write letters to her, explaining who they are and what they want, which is a wonderfully unique way to make your characters seem real. Another possibility is to 'sit down with your character' and ask questions about who they are, what secrets they are hiding, and what they want out of life. The writer's brain can make odd subconscious decisions in situations of this type.

Sometimes you cannot see what you really need until you are actually working on the story. Don't be afraid to change aspects of your characters, including the main character, after you start working on the novel. Always be certain to carry those changes through and rework any earlier part of your story which might now need to be changed as well.

What does the character want? A main character needs goals so he can strive to accomplish something. Such a goal may become apparent early in the story when the character faces some situation that he wants to correct. When you are considering the character, also ask yourself if you really think this is a character who would take up the fight. If not, then change those aspects of the character which you think don't fit. This doesn't mean the character has to be a born hero. Unexpected people are pushed into the role of hero every day. Just make certain your character is in a position to be pushed in the right way.

One last thing to remember about a main character who is also a 'hero' in the larger sense of the word: a hero is an everyday person pushed into extraordinary circumstances. While there might be a story to be written about a professional hero, it is more likely that he is still a regular guy (or gal) pushed into an unusual situation. So it is important to show that your main characters have all the good and bad parts which make us all human – or the alien equivalent.

What if...

A small colony on a world far from contact with Earth is faced with impending disaster. The local government is unable to deal with the problem. Who would be the most likely person to step forward and take charge? Who would be the least likely? What could either of these characters bring to the story to make it more interesting?

Creating villains

The first thing you need to do when you think about your villain is to dismiss the stereotyped visions of a megalomaniac genius bent on controlling or destroying humanity. Even if this is who your character ultimately turns out to be, you can't start with him fully formed because he won't seem real. Something made him as he is, and you need to work at discovering his background and building him as a fully-fledged human (or alien). Much like the problem with the voracious bug-eyed monsters, the age of the completely evil, soulless villain is over.

This may seem an unnecessary way to create antagonists for the story since we appear to live in an age of mindless rage and unreasoning acts of violence. However, most organized crime has a reason behind it and mindless crime rarely makes for a very satisfying story. Also, it is often true that fiction has to be more structured than real life and cannot get away with the coincidences and motiveless acts we find in the real world. Readers expect better than real life from their books and they want to understand the 'Why?' behind evil, even though this question cannot always be answered in the real world.

All characters spending any significant amount of time on the pages need to have motivation and background for what they do. This is probably more important for the villain than it is for the hero, who might simply be someone who is caught in unusual circumstances and forced into the role. If you are writing a story where one side is clearly in the wrong, then there needs to be a reason why that person has chosen the 'wrong' side.

Wrong, however, is sometimes an ambivalent state when viewed from two different perspectives. In a recent news story, the situation of a child bride seemed entirely wrong until it was pointed out that the parents were, at least in part, trying to make certain of a good future for their daughter who could be far worse off without a husband. The story was no less appalling, but a measure of understanding gave it new depth and made the viewer look into aspects that wouldn't have been obvious otherwise. In a poor country where unmarried women might not survive, making certain of a husband early in life could be viewed as a form of kindness from the parents.

So it is possible for two people to be opposed, and yet neither of them to be in the wrong. In such a story, it might be difficult to tell the 'good guy' from the 'bad guy.' This can be especially effective in a human versus alien tale, but only if you put a good deal of effort into creating an alien who can stand as an equal beside your human character.

Villains usually have the same sort of background as everyone else, but at some point their views and goals were twisted, until they began to slip out of the mainstream of what everyone else wants and instead began to view things in ways most people would not. The point where they changed can be obvious and a big event, or it can be a small single step that started showing them how they could be different from the crowd.

What your villain wants has to be logical within the framework of his own world. This doesn't mean a character can't reach beyond what he has, but he has to be able to comprehend and believe he could reach such a goal – unless he is delusional. A delusional villain can be unpredictable and dangerous, but the delusions still have to be able to tie with what he is doing in the 'real world' or else he won't be a danger to anyone but himself. If a villain wanted to reset the universe back to the Big Bang, the only way he could be a problem is if he had some sort of real power in his hands which might make him trouble at a local level, since plainly he would not have the power to accomplish his real goal.

Villains require the author to take special care to make them seem real to the reader. If you cloak your villain as a corporate entity, the reader still needs to believe that the people behind the company would allow things to happen the way they have for their own reasons. Those reasons can include greed, of course. However, faceless villains can be a problem when trying to create the conflict and goals of the hero. A hero's goal to 'destroy the corporation' only works if the reader believes the corporation has a heart to be destroyed. Companies are still made up of people and if you decide on some computer running the show, the computer will have to be sufficiently powerful – probably one imbued with artificial intelligence – to be a reasonable villain.

There are also stories which focus on man-against-nature. In those cases, the villain takes on the form of unreasoning nature. This is unlikely to be the only type of book an author would ever write, though, so working at villain creation will help for other books.

A villain can be no less complex than a hero; in some cases his motivations need to be even more carefully examined and understood.

> **What if...**
>
> Look back at the 'What if' exercise for hero creation and consider a character who might oppose a hero trying to help such a colony. Consider three different scenarios for this character:
> 1. He is the one creating the trouble.
> 2. He doesn't think the hero will help and fears the hero might make things worse.
> 3. He is jealous of the hero doing something that perhaps he himself should have done instead, but was too frightened to try.

Special problems with protagonists and antagonists

One problem writers face when they choose their hero (protagonist) and put him into the story is that they too often create a character who the surrounding events act upon, but who never steps forward with the initiative to take control and do something to change what is happening. This is a passive hero – everything happens to him, but he does nothing to fight back until he has to because he has no choice.

Readers will often lose interest in such a character who does nothing but react. While a hero can start out this way, at some point he has to step forward and take up the challenge, making decisions that affect what is happening in the story. He has to start directing the storyline by what he does, rather than what is pushed at him.

There is often a far different problem with the creation of villains. Let's take the example of an alien invader. He's the commander of a huge armed force and has advanced technology far superior to anything his enemies might have. So what is stopping him from reaching out and swatting the nuisance hero out of existence?

When creating the antagonist of a story, writers sometimes go over the top to make certain the villain is sufficiently bad enough to pose a real threat. Sometimes, however, they create someone so bad the reader is left wondering why he doesn't act on what he wants and be done with it.

Villains need to have limits. So do heroes, because it is possible to also create such a great, strong, perfect hero that the reader wonders why the hero doesn't just step in and fix everything. Or, conversely, either side can be made too weak, leaving the reader wondering why there is a problem defeating them at all.

It has to be a balance on both sides. It doesn't hurt for the villain to have the upper hand, which makes for a good fight by the hero against the odds. However, the villain cannot be so powerful that the only way the hero is going to win is if the villain does something stupid.

Another question you might want to ask is if your hero or villain was born a leader or if, on the other hand, he was pushed into a role to which he was unsuited. This can happen on either side of the good and bad line. Not everyone consciously chooses to continue along the path they first follow, though at some point they will make the choice to go on or to turn away.

Secondary characters

In most stories, the hero is leading and helping others. In such a group, there are usually one or two characters who are closer to the hero than the others. These secondary characters come in several forms: romantic interest, sidekick, second-in-command and even sibling. They need as much attention as you give to the main characters when you are creating who they are and what motivates them. In some stories it might be difficult to tell a secondary character from a main character and their roles may intertwine. Sometimes secondary characters surprise the author by demanding a larger role than expected in the story.

A romantic interest for the main character can add more than sexual tension to a story. This character, male or female, can be the trusted person to whom the main character admits fears, discusses plans, and generally relaxes their guard. A main character can be winning the battle but losing in love, which creates a kind of dichotomy that adds problems and more tension to a story. Romantic characters can also be the 'I thought we were just friends' type, which can add another twist to the story. And, of course, they can be the character who represents the worst kinds of betrayal.

A sidekick character often serves as the comic relief in a story – however, they are also the person who stands by the hero through all their travails. They are the ones whom the main character can entrust with any job, though they may not always succeed, which only reinforces why the hero is needed. There may be moments of doubt for the sidekick, but it is rare for a sidekick to change sides or to abandon his position.

A second-in-command need not be thought of in military terms. This is the person who is in charge whenever the main character is not available. They need not be a staunch supporter of the main character, though, and there may be tension over which one of them should really be in charge. Any business employing a few people will have a second-in-command who is the natural choice to keep things moving when the boss isn't around.

A sibling character can have a number of different roles to play, from sidekick to a problem created by the inherent rivalry between brothers and sisters. It is not unusual for someone to take a family member less seriously than a total stranger would, and this can create problems with respect issues. But siblings also share experiences and this can help create more depth and understanding when it comes to certain actions.

All of these characters can easily be added into most science fiction stories. Twists on the character types can be created for alien characters. For instance, relationships which might be straightforward for humans could mean something entirely different within an alien culture. As long as you work the reasons into the background for those characters, you can make nearly anything work in a science fiction story. So always look for the unusual and find ways to twist what might be expected.

Other characters

Books often have a plethora of characters moving on and off stage within a couple pages. Some of them impart important information while others are only there to give the place a lived-in look, rather than an empty stage. How much detailed work you put into creating these characters should be equal to the amount of story-work they are going to do for you. If all they are going to be is window dressing, then they can be mannequins. Dress them out nicely, stand them up in their places and don't worry about them.

When you start looking at extra characters, keep one important fact in mind: readers have a limited capacity to remember characters and you want them to focus on the important ones. Rather than taking time to create complex characters who are not going to be vitally important to the story, you would do better to take the time to work more on your worldbuilding or plotting.

There are some characters who are born to be the 'Red Shirts' of the stories – those characters who are there to be sacrificed at the first battle. Sometimes you don't want them to be anything more than the people in the line passing by – a face seen and gone, though perhaps remembered later when things don't go well. Other times, you might want to give those characters at least a paragraph or two to become sympathetic before they are killed off.

It's a difficult balance to find and there can be no single answer to fit all the instances when you have scenes of these types. The best I can do is to warn you not fill the pages with characters who are not going to be there after the end of the chapter. Mention crowds, mention lines of soldiers (or whatever else happens to work) and let the reader fill in much of the rest. Readers have excellent imaginations and they can see many things if you give them a few visual clues.

It is important to keep the amount of important characters down to a manageable number. Don't fall into the 'cast of thousands' problem. The reader won't be able to track them all, so focus on the people who are really important to the story.

> **What if...**
>
> Back at our colony facing a problem, the hero and villain are facing the same crowd. How do they each see the people? Who would they pick out from the crowd? What are the differences in how they react to the people? These are clues not only to who the people in the crowd are, but to the personality of who is looking at them.

Working with alien characters

One of the more difficult aspects of writing science fiction is to create a realistic alien character. If you have already done the worldbuilding part of the work, you've already begun creating a non-human society which will help you define your character. Now, however, you have to make an alien character seem real, which is far more difficult than with a human character. Writers can make readers understand the motivation and needs of a human character, even when such a character is outside the norm. But readers often want something *different* when it comes to a non-human.

There are two outside influences and one inner influence which combine when making characters of any type. These three things can be especially important when you are looking at how to make your aliens seems less human.

The first outside influence is culture, which defines everything from personal beliefs to the very words available within a language. Culture is partly formed by the world in which the character lives, while the form the alien character takes is influenced by the world. Everything is intertwined. Cultural influences will often dictate what a character wants in life. This means that worldbuilding to create the culture for an alien race is vital. Culture will also influence how the character deals with others. If the culture has a strict taboo about dealing with 'others' then it is going to be very difficult for the alien to work with humans, unless the humans can be somehow incorporated into his cultural group.

The second outside influence is the alien character's needs. These can be both physical and psychological. Needs are stronger than wants: we need air, water and food. Aliens will likely need similar items, but the more you can change these things (but still make them logical) the more *alien* your character will be, and the less human. The problem, as always with creating aliens, is that we are limited in defining them by human terms.

Motivation is the single inner influence which will come more from the character than from the other two influences. We all know people who are highly motivated to do something and others who are not. Often it seems as though outside influences have little to do with it. Someone who grows up poor, for instance, may be so highly motivated she'll work very hard to make a better life for herself, while her brother is content to continue following in their father's footsteps and work at the factory.

Motivation is the personal drive which each of your characters possesses, alien or not, and it directs their goals and dreams. Motivation is what will make the person cooperate with others towards some goal, or move against what the others want in another case.

An alien's motivation might not be the same as a human's would be in the same situation. Or perhaps it is the same, drawing the aliens and the humans together. These are the things the author has to decide.

Every time the author can tweak something to give slightly different than expected reactions, it will help to create a more interesting alien character. The tweaks have to add up to make a logical creation which lives by consistent rules already defined for him.

There is no simple way to create a believable alien character. It isn't as simple as adding extra arms, a pair of wings, different food needs and a shrill voice. If this is the description of the alien you want to create, you have to take each of those pieces apart, imagine the world in which the alien was created, imagine what life would be like there, how the aliens would interact, what needs and goals such aliens might have – and *then* you have to start considering how to make this particular alien a unique character among the other aliens who came from the same background. If your story only deals with one alien, then you have an easier time.

But if humans are ever going to encounter others of this alien species again, then you need to consider personality as an individual aspect of this character. If you already have a number of such aliens, then defining who they are as individuals is all the more important.

One excellent example of alien character creation is Brymn, a member of the alien Dhryn in Julie Czerneda's *Survival* which is the first book of the *Species Imperative* series. Brymn is an alien with a fully realized personality, an ability to interact with humans, yet he still maintains an air of difference which goes beyond the fact he doesn't look like a human. You cannot take shortcuts with any of your main and secondary characters, no matter what their background. It is important they fit into their world (unless you purposely don't want them to in some way) so your character – alien or human – needs to work credibly within the framework of your worldbuilding.

Using archetypes

Archetypes are characters representing certain aspects of humanity that can be recognized by others and easily understood. Using them can be especially helpful for creating symbolism or to explore mythical ideas. Some of the character types I've already mentioned, protagonist-hero, antagonist-villain and sidekick, are already understood as archetypes. There are many other types, more than I will mention here, and you might want to make a fuller study of this type of character creation.

Many of the other archetypes are taken up by secondary characters and they can be especially important for defining what these characters want or need to do within the story. You do not need to be writing a myth-based story to make use of these types of characters. They can help to define a character's interaction with others and their place within the story.

Mentor

Mentors are the ones who teach the characters what they need to know in order to succeed. They can be a parent, a commanding officer, a teacher or a wandering stranger. Creating a mentor character allows you to have a voice with which to impart important information and training, although the mentor is sometimes unaware of his or her role as such. A mentor can be someone from the past whose importance isn't understood until a critical time. Mentors can also be written so that they have the chance of failing at important points, forcing the main character to move on and learn the important truths by himself.

Threshold guardian

These characters stand between the main character and something he needs to have or do in order to succeed. They can be hiding knowledge or they can literally be guards standing at a door, stopping the main character from going inside. A friend can be a threshold guardian if the friend hides some truth in order to protect the character.

Passing a threshold guardian often is a sign of momentous progress within a story. It can also mark a change in status of the hero as he overcomes a difficulty. A villain's henchman is often a threshold guardian, as is a school bully who makes life difficult for the character.

Shapeshifter

A friend who turns on the main character and joins the enemy, or an enemy who saves your main character's life and comes over to the good side, both represent the shapeshifter archetype. Shapeshifters are the ones who can sometimes show both sides of the tale and in some cases it can be difficult to decide which side they are on. They can represent both betrayal and change – and they need not be evil.

Any of the characters around the hero or villain can be a shapeshifter. They can add tension and surprise to a story as they betray one side or the other.

Shadow

Shadows are the dark characters. In some stories they are represented by the villain, but in others they are the person working for the villain instead (possibly because the villain has a good reason for what he is doing). A secondary character serving the villain might have a darker side, being there solely for power, money or the chance to create havoc.

A paid killer would be a shadow archetype, as would be a second-in-command who keeps essential information from the villain, directing him to do something he might not have done if he had all the information (and this would also make that person a threshold guardian.)

Shadows are trouble. They relish creating trouble, especially if they are not going to have to take responsibility for it. They often work in the background – which fits their shadow status.

Trickster

Sidekicks are often tricksters. They can be amusing but can also create problems. Often they blur the sense of absolute right by creating a little ambiguity. A trickster might lead the main character astray, though usually not with truly malicious intentions.

Tricksters can sometimes see both sides of the story, so they might not be firmly committed to one side or the other. A trickster might be a go-between or he might be someone who leads authorities astray so that the villain's people can escape. In the case of a villain with a cause that is not entirely evil, this can help to keep the balance. Tricksters can also lay down false trails, give away important information at the wrong time, and generally create chaos.

So those are some main archetypes. Don't be afraid to play with the idea of archetypes as a basis for a character, but remember that such basics are merely stepping stones and making characters into individuals takes far more than deciding on a single quality. An archetype is only a title and no one is ever judged by a single quality.

> **What if...**
>
> What if you wanted to create an alien as an archetype? Yoda is a famous alien mentor, but what might it take to create an alien trickster or a threshold guardian? How could such a character remain alien and still fulfil an essential archetype function?

Soldier, baker, technoplasma light maker

People in the future will have jobs and will have learned certain skills just as we do today. The future may not always be filled with jobs the way we see them – nine to five, going to the office or the factory – but as long as there is work that needs to be done, someone will have to do it. Or, at the very least, someone will have to oversee the equipment doing the work. However, it is unlikely, especially if you are starting new colonies, that there will be enough income to import the technology which would make human workers superfluous.

This is an important part of creating characters. What their jobs have been in the past will influence what they know and how well they work with others. It also gives them a little more depth in ways readers understand. Characters with this kind of detailed background to call upon look less like they sprang into existence two minutes before the author started writing the book.

What will work be like in the future, though? There are bound to be changes from the sorts of jobs available today. This is the time to look back at your worldbuilding again, to see what sort of changes would affect jobs. Consider as many aspects as you can and see if you can parcel the work out among your top characters. If there is a push for people to move to new worlds, what kind of industries would this create? What weight requirements would limit the characters' belongings, what items could be compacted for the journey and what would need to be recreated at the new place? What would happen to items left behind? Who would study the group of people leaving and decide what additional skills they might need, and how best to either teach them to the settlers or hire the right people to go with them?

Would an aircar industry be much like the car industry? How about the building of robots, androids and the rest? How is food bought on the new world? For that matter, how is it grown and brought to market? Are there still farmers who work much the same as they have for the last couple of hundred years?

If you are writing a science fiction story about the future, how do the characters fit into their world? This is related to the culture of the time, but it is also a state of mind. We think differently than our ancestors did because our minds are occupied with things they never would have considered.

Today, the pursuit of food and shelter is usually limited to simplistic ideas of grabbing something at the store and getting home. These two primary goals, which have previously occupied most of human existence, normally don't take considerable time and effort. Instead, the time previously spent in those pursuits is now focused on a day job and relaxation. We still work for food and shelter, but not in the direct way that our ancestors did, which may have blunted some aspects of our overall survival instincts.

What will your people of the future pursue? What differences are there between the people on Earth and the people who have moved off to other colonies, where they might well experience a step back in history as far as survival is concerned?

We are not essentially different from our great-grandparents. We direct our survival instinct in a different way from those who had to go out and shoot dinner, or work on the land to bring in the crops. And they in turn were little different from our ancestors who went out and hunted with bows or clubs and who gathered nuts and berries from the wild fields. We may not have their basic skills in how to survive, but the same drive is still there. The difference is in how our culture has trained us to respond.

What if...

What survival challenges will your characters face which we do not have in the current world? How can you make your characters fit into the vision of your future? In what way can you make aliens have a different future than the humans?

Creating characters and spending time getting to know them are important steps in writing a good story. Whether you start with a plot first or the characters first makes no difference as long as you put enough effort into both parts. In this chapter we looked at many aspects of character creation, but the best way to make a character real and unique is to look beyond the superficial aspects and always ask yourself 'why' your character is where he or she is and what in the past brought the character to this spot.

In the next chapter, we'll look at aspects of plotting a story and some tricks to help keep the plot moving so your characters achieve their goals without getting lost along the way.

12 Pulling it All Together

- The work of writing the story
- Developing the background
- Titles
- Plotting the future
- Story creation
- Working with outlines
- How to keep stories moving forward

Now that you have created all the background material for your story, from actual worlds to aliens, cultures and characters, it is time to pull all the work together and make a coherent and exciting story out of it.

Having done the worldbuilding and character creation ahead of time can help, though if you are driven by the plot, rather than the characters, you may start working out the storyline and then do the character creation for each person as you add him into the story. As long as you give each character the full attention they need to work in the story, it doesn't matter what order you do the individual pieces in.

The work of writing the story

At some point every author has to move away from the excitement of worldbuilding and take the next step toward writing. Don't let yourself get caught in the trap of continual worldbuilding and never moving on to the story itself. It can be a seductive trap as you create world after world, building cities and spaceships, fashioning intricate cultures and creating the fascinating characters that exist in these places.

But writing the story is the real goal and it is as much fun as creating all the background material. In the last chapters of this book, we're going to cover some simple ways to help you write the science fiction novel or story you want to tell. Much of what is covered in these final pages can be applied to books of other genres as well.

Stories have essentially three interwoven aspects: world, character and plot. The world is everything from the actual world to the furniture in the character's living room. All of it is background material; if you have done your pre-work properly, it will all fit together so it seems natural, even if it is a completely alien setting.

Characters, as we have already learned, are creatures of their background. But they are also children of the author's heart and soul. The author can fill in the blanks of a dozen character sheets and still not have characters that come alive on the pages. The author has to breathe life into each one, moving them carefully like a director does in a movie, rather than manipulating them roughly as though they were puppets on strings.

Plot is what your characters do to work their way through the problems the author has set up for them. They will interact with each other and with the environment, they will confront each other, and they will fail sometimes and win other times. But as long as they keep moving forward, toward the ending that the author has in mind, they are working with the plot. If, however, they go off on their own adventures, in which the author pretends not to have any control, then the plot becomes a confused mess.

Characters are always in the control of the author. When someone says the characters didn't follow the plot and headed off in their own directions, what that really means is something in the plot did not satisfy the author, who began to explore other ideas. Sometimes this can work and results in a more interesting storyline. Other times it creates problems which can never be solved and the story is abandoned.

The heart of plotting is to create problems for your characters. These cannot be random troubles, though. They have to interlock with the world and the other characters in the story. For instance, the antagonist must want something related to the world in which he exists, and the protagonist must have a good reason for wanting to stop him from attaining his goal. Or, of course, it could be the other way around: your protagonist has a goal, either for himself or for others, but the antagonist feels strongly about stopping our hero!

Also, the basic trouble has to be big enough to matter. If the story is how the protagonist doesn't want the rude guy he works with from getting the job as the head of the robo department, is the reader really going to care? It might make an entertaining short story, but if you want something with more depth then you need to increase the tension and the trouble.

For the remainder of this book, I am going to work through a single novel-length story idea so we can examine concrete examples of how these pieces will work and how to pull them together. These will usually be short versions of the full material to give you an idea of how to manipulate your information and create a story out of it.

> **What if...**
>
> After having read this book up to this point, you probably have some idea of the type of story you would like to write. Write out a short description, no more than a paragraph long. This will be your primary guide to what your book is to be about – but you can edit it as many times as you need to while the idea clarifies in your mind.

Developing the background

Everything we have looked at so far in this book has dealt with different elements of storytelling, such as how to build your world and create your characters. Now we'll look at how to pull all these pieces together and make a coherent story out of them.

Many writers, especially new ones, leap straight into the story without doing any of the background work first. Sometimes they get lucky and have a gift for pulling the story together anyway. Often, however, they find themselves floundering in a sea of possibilities and with no clear idea of how to get anywhere, let alone to a reasonable closure for the story.

Writing full, entertaining stories is an art form and, like all other arts, you cannot expect to do well without practice. Books like this one can only give you some ideas of how to approach the work; in the end, you have to find your own way. What works for some people will not work for others. The best other writers can do is show you what works for them, but you have to find ways to apply their advice to your own methods.

If you have gone through this book and used it as a basis for finding information you will need, the chances are you now have a number of notes on everything from star types to cultural eating habits. But those notes are likely to be a chaotic mess at the moment and difficult to work with.

The first thing is to divide your notes into sets to make it easy for you to view and manipulate them. Some of the notes you've made may overlap. If you have written these on paper or note cards, you can either mark which ones belong to two groups or copy the piece and put it into both groups. This sorting is far easier to do on the computer, of course, where you can copy/paste items into whatever section you want them in.

The example story will be about a sleeper ship (cryogenic or stasis field) heading for a new world which is several hundred years away. The ship's computer will pilot the craft to a planet, make certain of the world's viability, and begin the process of waking the passengers.

In this story, when the main character finally wakes up she learns the ship encountered a problem but aliens helped save it with the help of some awakened crew. They found a world and those awakened crew and their descendants have been settled there for more than 200 years. The sleepers are waking to a world in turmoil and their help is needed. Unfortunately, they feel as though they don't fit in.

In order to make sense out of the background material I have created, I will need my material divided into these groups:

- The world (including sun, plants, weather, etc.)
- Settler humans and their culture
- Sleeper humans and their culture
- Aliens and their culture
- Characters

What I write for these examples will be nothing more than the bare essentials of what would really be necessary to write the book properly. If I wrote everything out, it would take far more space than is available in this book!

The world

In this section, put anything to do with the world itself. If you are writing about Earth, then you would make note of any changes brought about by the time frame addressed in the book. If you are writing about another world, then you would put in any of the notes about the world, whether it is Mars or some world you've created.

Once again, it's important to consider what you want out of this setting and tailor your world to meet those expectations. If you want to stay on Earth, but you want it to be different than the world of today, look closely at the possibility of physical change and how it will affect people.

If you are moving off Earth, include the unusual in your descriptions. If you are going to write about a world that is like Earth, make certain it has some obvious differences. Readers want to know they are 'visiting' another world.

For my story, a simplified version of the world would be something like this:

An F1 sun, which would appear more orange than the Earth's sun. The world would orbit a bit closer than Earth does to our sun. It would not be enough to make the sun appear noticeably larger, but would make it a slightly different colour.

I am calling my world Ostara, after the Germanic goddess of spring and fertility, and the name suits at least the settlement area where the humans are located. The world has 79% of Earth's gravity, giving it towering mountains and tall plants, but this will make exploration beyond the original valley somewhat difficult, especially in the first couple of generations. There are large ice caps at both poles and a circumpolar sea in the north. Several more oceans, including inland seas, are spread over the world, dividing the five large continents and several small island groups. The world is closer to the sun, so it has a shorter year. Since the settlement is near the equator, there is no real winter but they do suffer through a rough rainy season.

Two small satellites, close together and part of what had been a larger object, orbit Ostara with a trail of rubble behind them. Some of the rubble occasionally falls down to the planet in the form of meteorites, though most of the larger pieces fell very soon after the original satellite broke apart, so what comes down now is relatively small and harmless, and most of it is stable. The moons exert enough gravitational pull to affect the tides.

There is a lovely blue and red nebula in the southern half of the sky (as seen from the equator, where the settlement is) and a large red giant star hangs to the north of it. The Milky Way is a little more visible, though high up on the northern horizon.

The plants and native animals mostly seem to be larger than what would be found on Earth, but with a more fragile structure. Some of the animals have a triple eye system, a few have lush pelts, but for the most part they seem to have a hide or scaly covering.

Settler humans and their culture

Defining the general background for the world in which your characters move will help provide the walls of your story. This does not mean your story will stay within those walls, but it will help your reader to know what is normal and what is not. The readers need to see those walls in order to make judgement calls about what is going on, especially in a genre like science fiction where the premise might include changes so strange the reader couldn't begin to guess what the norm might be.

You do not, however, have to overload the start of the book with all this information. You can either make it plain from the way others react, or you can gradually lead the reader to understand when something out of the ordinary happened.

Here are a few notes for the settler culture:

The oldest of this group is already four generations removed from Earth and the rest of the sleepers. Because of the damage to the ship and their connection to the aliens, they have little knowledge of Earth.

The largest percentage of the group was not made up of technically-skilled people, but rather farmers and others who were needed to settle the new world. The people who were awakened from 'sleep' aboard the ship were chosen haphazardly, based mostly on whether the aliens felt certain pods were failing or not. Half of them didn't survive awakening, so the aliens were worried about trying to awaken any of the others. This situation was not helped by the fact that the humans and aliens didn't understand each other and so the aliens didn't know what the humans needed.

A generation died on the ship, but the next generation, helped by the aliens, found the world and set about making the colony. Because some of their supplies were destroyed during the trouble on the ship, the settlers left the rest of the sleepers as they were. They knew it would take a while before the new world could support more than the original small group.

The settlers have had contact with the aliens and, because of the close quarters on the ship, had already picked up several alien cultural habits and pieces of the language, which they carried over to the new settlement. They bow with hands to their eyes, they eat kneeling, and they sometimes wear a covering which looks much like the carapace of the aliens.

By the third generation, there was a question about whether or not the sleepers should be awakened at all. Many of the settlers felt that the world should be theirs alone and, since the sleepers wouldn't know one way or another, it didn't hurt to leave them where they were. Some wanted to destroy them, which divided the colony into protectors and protesters. But when the ship's power source starts to fail, one character takes matters into his own hands and awakens them.

The settlement itself is a growing set of concentric circles where the settlers have pushed outwards to gain a little more control of the land around them. Within these circles is where the Earth plants and animals are thriving. A few have escaped into the outside world, some of which survived. The locals do use many local plants, especially for building.

Culturally, they have adopted an odd combination of alien gestures and words, along with close knit family groups based on a matriarchal line, and some hold a belief in Earth technology which verges on religion. They know what the ship did and they know it still holds secrets, but the only keys they have to unlock those secrets are the sleepers. Some of the settlers have tattoos which mimic the carapace designs of the aliens.

Sleeper humans and their culture

If you have created two groups, then you want to define them in ways that show they are different from one another. This does not mean they have to be opposites, but they need to diverge in ways that make each group unique. Customs, beliefs and etiquette are good ways to show those differences.

Here are some notes for the second group:

The sleepers left Earth believing they would awaken to a new world, far outside Earth control and beyond their home world's growing problems with war, pollution and inability to support the population.

They were 1,000 strong on the ship with an advanced computer that would seek out the perfect world for them and do whatever work was needed to make the world viable for settlement.

Of the 1,000 who took to the ship, only 223 actual sleepers finally awaken on their new world. There they find they will have no say in anything about how the world is set up since the settlement is long past such a stage. The work they had trained for is already done. They've been pulled out of sleep rather than left to die. Also, the settlement is facing problems and some there think the sleepers can help.

They are very much an Earth-based cultural group. They came on this journey knowing they would have a hard time on a new world but they brought technology with them to put up a good fight. But now they are awakened far later in the settlement than they expected and most of their technology is already compromised in one way or another.

They do not fully understand the other humans, with whom they come into conflict in a number of areas, especially around rules and customs.

Aliens and their culture

Creating an alien culture takes a great deal more work than creating human cultures. It is easy to fill in the blanks when you start working with human cultures. Aliens, whether human-like or not, need to have more twists and turns in their background.

This is some of my background work on the aliens:

The aliens are the mystery element in this story. Although the aliens had found the ship, they were never forthcoming about whether they knew how it was damaged. Even several generations later, it's obvious the craft was cut open by something... but it might not have been the aliens who had first helped them. The settlers had the impression of a war.

Another impression the settlers got from the aliens was that they had to decide whether to let everything in the ship die or to try to save the people on it. They decided it would be wrong to turn their backs on the people in need, and besides they were intrigued by the new race.

The aliens themselves are somewhat squat, short-legged, bipeds with two arms, but also with two auxiliary arms used for climbing and sometimes in battle. These arms are located within the indentions of a carapace which covers the body from back of head to mid-leg in the back and from chin to the same location in front. It is hinged in three places – mid-chest, waist and halfway down the leg – and the body within has considerable bending and twisting ability at each of those sections. The carapace is very hard, though thin, and is often decorated with various designs that the settlers assume are emblems of status.

The face is dominated by huge dark eyes that can be protruded far enough to see almost completely behind them without turning the unprotected face. There is no nose and the mouth is also protractible, though normally it appears as a thin slit at the bottom of the face, with very little chin area beneath.

The main arms end with multiple feelers, something like thin fingers with many joints. Half of them end with suction cups and the others with needle-like nails. The humans believe the needles hold some kind of poison.

The humans know very little about the aliens' home world. They assume it is brighter and hotter, based on what they know from the few who had visited the alien ship. Gravity is stronger than on Earth. The aliens eat some plant-like growths. They are startled by birds, suggesting there may not be any flying creatures on their world.

Characters

Making a list of the main characters will help to define where they belong in the story. Like all the other sections here, I will provide a bare outline of the extensive material which would be needed to explore this topic fully. Each character would likely have a page or more of information, and this listing would grow and change during the writing process.

Here are some of the characters for the story:

The first POV (point of view) character will be Felicia Aznar, who was intended to head the group when they found a world on which to settle. She's 30, Hispanic, and a successful scientist – but so dedicated to her work that she's been divorced twice. She didn't find it difficult to leave Earth, family and her few friends for the chance to be the head of what she considers to be the ultimate science experiment. Awakening only after the experiment is already several generations old, she knows all her original plans and work are useless now. She's lost, uncertain what to do and unclear about what the settlers want from her and *her* people.

The second POV character is Jasha Mar Leodora – which means he traces his ancestry from Leodora Payne, who was one of the sleepers woken by the aliens. He is a combination mayor and go-between with the aliens. He is also clearly on the side of the protectors (those who wanted the sleepers brought into the community) rather than a protestor (those who wanted the sleepers destroyed, rather than let in where they might take over). This puts Jasha in conflict with a large section of his own people, but also gives him a position of power because of his link to the sleepers as someone they trust. He is also the official speaker to the aliens, giving him even more opportunities for power and trouble.

The main alien character is Ererra (mostly pronounced with rolling r sounds) who arrives at the settlement with a few companions not long after the sleepers are awakened. The alien does not have a POV part in the story, but observation of him will lead to some understanding of what is going on. Ererra seems to be running from something and his contact with the other aliens is brief, terse and filled with words and actions Jasha and others have defined as troubling. He has three companions, but they seem to be little more than caregivers and servants.

Other characters will be sleepers and settlers. Sleepers are greatly outnumbered, but they do have some technical knowledge that will help repair neglected systems on the downed ship, which had been made to withstand just about anything.

What if...

If you have done any of the pre-writing work suggested earlier in the book, what sections would you use for your story? If you have not, try to imagine what might be important to you. Sections that I did not cover, for instance, are government, technology and ecology.

Titles

There is one subject I have purposely skipped until now: how to title your work. I have done this on purpose because too many people place far too much importance on finding the right title before they start the work.

This is pointless as you never know when the publisher is going to decide your title is not the one the book will actually have when it is published. If you get too attached to a title, you can be disappointed by the time the story sees print. A title is only a few words, but it is the story itself that the reader will make a real decision on.

There are some things you can do to come up with a working title if one hasn't yet occurred to you. If you hope the title remains, keep this in mind: a book title will usually be short because there is not much space on the spine of a book. The longer the title, the smaller the print will be, so you want something short and catchy.

Short stories can get away with longer titles, though. They do not usually appear on a book spine or cover, and magazine publishers are far more forgiving of something long and unusual. Take a look at some of Harlan Ellison's short stories for examples of long and interesting titles.

Let's look at book titles, then, since they have constraints. The first step is to figure out something significant about your book. This might be in the form of an object, a theme or a character name. If you can't come up with anything else, consider something like *Journey* for a working title until something better comes along.

In the case of the story I'm using as an example in this book, I decided to try something different. I thought of two words which are important to the story: journey and stars. I could go with something simple like *Journey to the Stars*, but I think this might be somewhat misleading. Sleeping is also a big part of the story so *Sleeper's Journey* or *Sleepers Awake* might work. *Broken Journey* might work better. For the moment, I'm going with *Broken Journey* because it suits the feel of the story. This is a title to help me while I'm working. Something better might come along later as I work through the book.

Don't let the lack of a good title hold you back from writing the story. People sometimes use this as an excuse to not get started on their book. If they never quite find the right title (or name of a character) it can stop them from ever writing the book at all. When you find yourself stopped by something like this, consider these two things:

First drafts are a gift to writers, and you never have to show the work to anyone.

The only story you can't fix is the one you never write.

Plotting the future

Once you have your ideas and notes arranged, you are ready to sit down and plot out the main points of your novel. Chances are you have had a lot of ideas about this already. You may have jotted a few of them down and perhaps written out a scene or two. Having all your background work done will make writing this book far easier than if you had to stop and make basic decisions about science, culture and characters every time you started a new scene. It also means you will have cohesion, not confusion, throughout the story.

You will most likely still hit a few spots where you need to clarify some of the work you've already done, but with the basics in place you will get through these problems.

Now that it's time to start working out the plot of the story, you might want to consider a theme. In a simple form, the theme is a single word describing a feeling which pervades the story. Some possible themes for *Broken Journey* might be discovery, loss or ambition. Various characters might work under different themes, but if you can assign one word as a unifying element, you have another tool to help with the work of writing the book.

For *Broken Journey* I'll use *trust* as the word. This single word will help me direct some of the scenes to mirror the theme as trust is given, misused or lost. The idea of trust will pervade the storyline and any time I have a problem directing a scene, I can look to the idea of trust as a key factor to get it moving again.

There may be other words I find work as themes as well. By adding them to a short list (no more than four or five) and assigning different ones to various characters or groups, I can have an easy reference to help direct the book forward again.

Although this book is about writing science fiction, no story is ever completely one made up of one genre. A science fiction novel might also be a mystery, romance, thriller, comedy, adventure or any other genre combination. So take advantage of the best that other genres have to offer. Learn how to tell a good mystery story or the tricks of writing a satisfying romance tale, even if those are not the main focus of your story. Almost all stories are quests of some type, whether the plot involves finding something specific or finding an answer to a question. Using some of the tricks from fantasy, including mythic and folk tale symbolism, can expand a science fiction tale with new areas that readers can relate to.

Story creation

Actually sitting down and working out the plot of a story before you write it is something authors sometimes find difficult to do. This type of work takes practice and can also require a change in attitude.

Having an idea of where your plot is going does not mean you have to write a traditional outline for your story, which might be too restrictive for your style of writing. However, you do need to know, in general, what you want out of the story. If you do not have any plan, chances are far better you'll get lost somewhere in the middle, get frustrated, and never finish the work. If this sounds like a familiar pattern of how your own work has gone in the past, then you need to jot down a few basic ideas of how the story should move forward from one major section to another. This need not be detailed – though if you enjoy writing detailed outlines, those work very well too.

This is an important art to learn. Publishers and agents usually want to see this type of material before the author writes a book so they can see if it is publishable. This saves the author from spending months on a book which can't find a market. The author is not tied to every step of the submission package, though. Publishers and agents understand that a story will mutate in some way between the pre-work and the final written manuscript.

There are several ways to divide up a story into sections. One of the easiest to work with corresponds to the three act system well known in playwriting. For this method, the story is divided into three parts: Opening, Middle and End. This division works as well for short stories as it does for novels. It can even provide the basics for a trilogy.

Here are the opening, middle and end ideas for *Broken Journey*:

Opening

The main character awakens to find someone standing over her – someone she does not know, a strange-looking human male with long hair, a triangle and line tattoo under his right eye, and wearing clothes that didn't come from the ship.

The sleepers were awakened because the ship's power systems were failing. The people who are now awakened are shocked and dismayed to learn that the ship was damaged and some of the passengers were revived long ago while still in space. With the help of the aliens, those passengers established a new world. They have been here for three generations, plus one generation which died on the ship.

Trouble erupts between sleepers and settlers, this isn't helped by the arrival of a small group of aliens who are shocked to find the sleepers awake and who seem to be hiding something.

The opening will deal with interaction, learning to trust each other and trying to find out what has gone wrong.

Middle

Settlers and sleepers find themselves increasingly at odds while another problem, in the form of alien spacecraft, begins to appear. They learn there is a growing war between this group of aliens and the ones who have been helping them. The settlers easily choose which side they will take, but the sleepers are not as easily won over.

Sleepers repair some of the ship's technical equipment, including weapon systems and computers. They are able to pull up computer video images of how the ship was damaged. This was done by a shot from a craft manned by the aliens who are now helping them.

Ererra, the alien, confesses his people thought the human craft had been a new enemy ship and that they had acted out of fear and haste. Since then they have done the best they could to make up for their mistake.

The sleepers also repair computer links and are able to see things the settlers never did, including the video of their coming to this world, which shows a vast settled continent half a world away. This turns out to be a settlement of the friendly alien group, who cannot settle where the humans have because the dampness causes a softening of the carapace and a rotting fungus. This revelation alerts the sleeper scientists to the problem with their failing crops.

Ending

Sleepers and settlers finally agree to help the aliens, who are surprised to discover that the humans have far higher technology than they first realized, having never seen any of it in use. Together they drive away the unfriendly aliens.

Sleepers, knowing they will never fit into this settlement that has gone on so long without them, ask aliens to help them resettle on the other side of the mountain where they can start from scratch, retaining all the original mission plans that they still believe in. A few of the settlers go with them and with the help of the friendly aliens they know they can stay in touch with the older settlement.

One thing to note about this kind of broad look at the story is it very rarely dwells on the individual people involved. It is purposefully left simple and there is no reason why large parts of it can't change as you write. This is nothing more than a directional guide to remind the author of where the story should head and what major points need to be covered.

> **What if...**
>
> If you have done any of the pre-writing work suggested earlier in the book, what sections would you use for your story? If you have not, try to imagine what might be important to you. Sections that I did not cover, for instance, are government, technology and ecology.

Working with outlines

An outline is only a roadmap: it will help direct your characters where they should go, but will not cover everything they see and do. The possession of this roadmap also allows for side-trips and detours without wrecking the story idea, because the author always has the map in hand and can find a path back to the main plot.

An outline traces the actions of your characters from the start of the story until the end. Every time a character makes a major step in some direction, the author should document it. This might be the outline for the opening scene of *Broken Journey*:

1. Felicia Aznar (POV1) awakes slowly, feeling the loss of what she has given up and fearing failure, before she realizes she is on a new world. She is shocked at seeing a face she doesn't recognize.
2. Demands to know what is going on, and realizes this stranger is having trouble understanding her. She slows down, and begins to understand. Been 'sleeping' for a long time.
3. Anger. Why not awakened? Others hear her voice and stumble in to see what is going on. The stranger starts looking worried, bows to leave – but others stop him. Felicia steps in and helps him, knowing it is the better way to get an answer.
4. Stranger introduces himself as Jasha Mar Leodora. Takes the group to the airlock, which is open and overgrown with vines. Looks with dismay out on a large village. Too much time has passed.
5. Anger from the villagers. Jasha awakening them was apparently not the plan.

A plot, however, isn't simply about movement. You must always add in points about the conflict as well. In these five short lines there are several spots of conflict:

> Felicia starts out angry and confrontational.
>
> Other sleepers are confused and upset, causing trouble for Jasha.
>
> Villagers are upset to find sleepers awake.

Outlines can be used to trace several other story aspects besides the obvious plot. In the case of a mystery (and many novels are mysteries in one way or another) you can track when and where you place important clues, allowing you to see who is present at each spot and to make certain the clues fall in a logical order.

You might also track how theme plays into each scene, checking to see if you can work some aspect of it into each section. You can come back after you have written the outline and see if you can tweak it a bit to cover more of the theme.

Outlines allow the introduction of subplots which follow their own listing of events. In a case like *Broken Journey* a subplot might follow minor characters from both human groups who are trying to work together to find an answer to a failing crop problem. Another might track a single settler who feels awakening the sleepers jeopardizes his position as the head of the almost religious-like cult of scientists who have passed scientific information down from parent to child from the few scientists who were awakened aboard the ship after the accident.

In both of those cases, there is ample room to use the 'trust' theme and to explore the culture of the settlers, who are obviously going to be the more interesting of the two human groups.

It might also help to keep an actual timeline tacked onto each chapter section. This can help the author make certain the actions are happening in a reasonable time frame. How long will it take for someone to get from one area of the settlement to another? Is it possible for a person to be present at two different events, or do you need to tweak the story so either more time passes, or the events are closer together physically, or the person learns about one of the events from someone else who was present.

If you do need more time to pass, you cannot add anything that comes to mind into the plot to cover it. The time has to connect the two pieces of information. There can be nothing in a story which doesn't further the plot and help to better define the story in some way.

If you have multiple point of view (POV) characters in the story, making note of who is the scene's POV character for each chapter or section can help the author decide if one character isn't getting enough material. The POV character is the one who is the focus of the story at that point in the manuscript. For example, in some chapters we might follow Felicia and in others we follow Jasha, in which case they would be alternating POV characters.

You may also want to track the actions and positions of characters who are not always present in the story. Just because Jasha Mar Leodora isn't in a scene doesn't mean he no longer exists in the story universe. What is he doing during that time? By tracking the actions of other characters, you can easily manipulate the characters so that not only do they appear where you want them to be when you need them in the story, but also because they have a good reason for being there.

Conflict is the essential fuel for a story. But conflict does not mean physical fights or shouting matches. In *Broken Journey*, Felicia might find herself fighting with her conscience as she tries to decide which group she should help. The sleepers are her people – people she trained with, people who had committed themselves to establishing a new world forever cut off from Earth. The settlers, however, plainly need her help. If there is trouble between the two groups – and of course there would be – Felicia might find it difficult to decide what she should do. The inner turmoil she feels is conflict.

Not everything has to be confrontational and troublesome, of course. Moments of calm help to accentuate the trouble, giving readers a 'roller-coaster' feel when they are reading a book.

Writing any sort of an outline – whether a list of general ideas, one or two lines per chapter, or a detailed scene-by-scene list of events – will help you track the storyline and make certain everything and everyone is in the right place. It will also help you catch some of the major story problems before they make it to the actual pages, where they will be far harder to correct.

While writing an outline, you can move forwards and backwards through the entries, adding and changing things as you work out some of the more intricate storylines. This also keeps the more easily tracked problems from making it to the story itself.

Outlines allow you to jump around in the story in ways you might not be so comfortable doing if you didn't have one, as sometimes it's hard to track who is where at any given time. This is especially true for non-linear writers, those who jump around in the story as they write it. By contrast, a linear writer starts at the first page and moves through the story to the end like a movie unfolding. They can jump around in the outlining phase as possibilities occur to them, which will help them to better define earlier scenes.

Outlines are used to experiment with the story. They allow you to trace the steps of something odd, so you can see if it will work. If so, it stays in the outline. If not, you can delete the section. This is (again) far easier than doing the same when actually writing the story.

Don't be afraid of outlines. They're a wonderful tool and can help you expand and experiment without the frustration of having to tear a finished story apart when something doesn't work. They need not be complex to be helpful.

Sometimes writers fear they are not making a proper outline. Outlines are for your own use only and you will not be turning them in for a class assignment. So it doesn't matter how you put these outlines together, as long as they work to help you create a better story.

It helps to drop notes into outlines to remind yourself of things you want to check. Is the date right for this event? If this is the half way point of the outline, is the novel word count also near the half way point? You can also add in those wonderful bits of dialogue that come out of nowhere, that you don't want to forget.

Outlines, whether traditional or a series of odd notes, will help you avoid moments when you can't decide how to move forward with the story. If you can see the path, you can push ahead. You might not take the exact trail you created with your outline, but you have a direction and a goal to reach and these will help you get through the book.

Outlines can be written on computer or on note cards. In both cases, the elements can easily be shuffled around, new pieces added in, and others rejected without too much trouble.

Sometimes when you reach the story-writing phase, you find a few of the scenes you outlined no longer work in the story. Don't feel an obligation to write the material just because you did the preparatory work. When you get to the writing itself, how the story flows has to hold the greater influence.

> **What if...**
>
> What type of outline would you feel most comfortable with? What would you track other than the plot of the story? Try working out the first scene of a story idea and see what appeals to you. You don't need to write all the details and you don't have to worry about it being 'right' yet. Outlines are vehicles of exploration.

How to keep stories moving forward

Knowing how to write an outline does not help if you don't know what to put in one. The ability to see stories unfold comes from inspiration and practice. Chances are your first science fiction novel will take far more work than later ones because, like all forms of art, you will get better with practice. Writing is a form of art: you are painting backgrounds and sculpting characters with words.

The first step in writing your outline is to imagine your opening scene. Quite often this scene will be something happening in the very heart of the initial trouble. With

Broken Journey I could have started with the ship leaving Earth, but that really isn't part of the story. It's background which can be worked in easily enough. An opening scene, fully written (rather than outline) might look like this:

> *Felicia came awake with ragged breaths, her memories sharp of her last waking moment. She had slipped into the pod on a ship soon to leave Earth, knowing she would be there for at least a hundred years or more, and knowing she would awake on another world. Now, with adrenaline and understanding surging through her, she blinked several times and focused –*
>
> *On a stranger.*
>
> *There should be no strangers on the ship.*
>
> *Something had gone wrong.*

With an opening like this one, I can get straight into the heart of the story, which is *not* about this group leaving Earth but rather about them awakening to find something they never expected and are not prepared to deal with.

In some cases, starting the novel too early can actually help. If I had started on Earth, I could have played with the personalities of the characters and come to understand them a little better, before I got to the real story. Starting too early would mean cutting several thousand words off the beginning of the story later, but it could give the author a little time to get used to the characters and to feel comfortable with the setting and story. The author may not be able to tell he or she has started too early. Sometimes it takes another reader to point that out.

When you are outlining, start the story where you think the most interesting action is taking place. Don't worry if the reader may not fully understand what is going on. If you start out the story with something interesting, the reader will stick around long enough to figure out the rest. However, if you start with a dull recitation of facts about your world or ship, the reader isn't going to be interested in what else is going on.

Once you get the idea of the opening down, there are only a few things you need to remember as you work through the rest of the story. The first is to make certain your main character really is carrying the majority of the story. The second is to decide what you want from this story. If the story is about an epic battle, do you want your main character and his allies to win? If so, what do they win? What do they sacrifice in order to win?

The opening is where you introduce the characters, the background and the problems facing the characters in order to reach a certain goal. All these elements have to be introduced as part of the story and not as though the author is listing facts. In *Broken Journey*, Felicia's goal was always to settle a new colony and start a new world. This may seem impossible now at the start of the book, but by the end of the book she will have found a way to make the goal real by taking some of her followers and moving across the mountains to found a new settlement. Setting up this 'failed' goal at the start of the book will help to define her attitude and frustrations.

Some writers fear the middle of the story. They have a good idea of what they want at the start and they can see the ending, but there is a vast, trackless desert in the middle of the book and they have no idea how to cross it.

But middles are really wonderful sections of the story to write. You are past the introduction of your characters and world, but are not yet moving toward the inevitable ending. In the middle stage, your characters can learn truths they would rather not know, have doubts and make mistakes. Your plot can veer from the straight path as your characters try to solve problems or are purposely led astray. This is the section of the book where the author may find the chance to do something odd even though it isn't in the outline.

The middle is where most of the story action will take place. It is the place where your characters face their hardest setbacks, where they make interesting new friends and where they doubt their own abilities. The middle is where false paths end, and where the story begins to narrow towards the ending confrontation.

Endings have their own problems. Aside from making certain the ending is powerful enough to please the reader, there is also the situation where the author goes too far. Sometimes it's difficult to let go and say *The End*. You do not want to continue too long after the last major confrontation. A denouement – which is a short section that follows the climax – might give an idea of how life is affected some time later, but such a section shouldn't be more than a couple of pages long.

Tie up all your loose ends at the end of the novel. Make certain you have accounted for everyone: for instance, don't leave the reader wondering about the five-legged alien sent off to find out where the enemy kept their weapons hidden.

Make certain your ending is a logical extension of the story and as powerful as the story had promised it would be. You cannot give a weak ending to a story which promised a confrontation full of fireworks and angst.

Moving from one step in a story to the next can be frustrating, both in the outline and in writing, if you find yourself uncertain about what to do next. There is, however, one easy question you can ask whenever you find yourself stuck in a story: *What is the worst thing that could happen now?*

Bad things are not always cataclysmic. A neighbour showing up at the wrong time can be a major problem, as can a request for a character to talk with their commanding officer. Storms, stalled cars, missing IDs – these are the types of smaller catastrophes that an author can add to a much bigger problem.

The important part is to keep the problems in context with the story. Anything you can tie into the bigger problem that will create more trouble for your characters is a potential way to create a fast-moving plot and will keep the reader turning the pages.

Creating obstacles your characters have to overcome, and through which they can learn something important, takes practice. Outlines help because you can trace out possible story ideas and see how you can tie them back into the main plot. You can pick up a problem, let it rest for a while, and then bring it back again in a way which makes it apparent this 'little thing' is far more of a concern than it first appeared to be.

Everything you write must help the story move forward in some way. You cannot have your characters get into trouble just to cause trouble. Your story isn't real life: most books have to make sense, where in real life *things happen* for no reason at all. A story might have a situation or two like this, but if the story is littered with problems that have nothing to do with the plot it looks as though the author has no idea what he or she is doing.

> **What if...**
>
> If you have an idea for a story, write three short paragraphs describing its beginning, middle and ending as you see it right now. (Don't worry if you don't think the idea has enough punch. The first step to writing a good story is understanding its walls and edges. It is useful to see the limitations the story idea places on all the myriad of possibilities out there before you define those boundaries.)

Once you have created the background material for a story, settling down and writing the material can be difficult if you haven't sorted your notes and begun processing the ideas into a story concept. However, with the help of a simple outline, you can begin to make a coherent plan for writing.

In the next chapter, we'll look at setting up goals, working on edits and some of the other steps that go into producing a solid, professional story – as well as knowing when it is time to let go and move on.

13 Working Like a Professional

- Setting goals and making schedules
- Writing, rewriting and editing
- Edit now or later?
- Getting outside help
- Two questions to ask about the story
- Checking the story one last time

Once you have all your background worked out and a plan of what you want to write, it is time to move on to doing the writing itself. With a few plot ideas in hand (or an entire outline) you can begin working through your story. This chapter will cover a few things which can help you make it to the end of the book.

Setting goals and making schedules

Short story writers have a relatively easy time of it when it comes to producing material. Not only is their work less likely to take years to produce, they aren't going to be faced with a worry new novelists often fear most: the two-book contract. Most publishers, if they accept one book, will have a clause in the contract saying they get a second book. This is so that if the first book is a hit, they have a chance at the next book as well.

The problem is that the second book often comes with a 'due date' attached. For someone who spent ten years perfecting their first novel, the idea of writing another one and turning it in within a year can look both insane and impossible.

In some cases, the contract can be rewritten. However, there is a good reason to try to get the second book written and on the shelf. Fans have thousands of new books thrown at them every year. You want them to remember your name. But if too much time passes between books, people are less likely to look at the name on the book and associate it with something they liked.

Many writers have written more than one manuscript before they sell their first novel, so it's sometimes not as difficult as it sounds.

If, however, the author is going to write a full second book in a year, then he needs to learn how to focus and get the work done. The trick, as with any work of this type, is to make goals and stick with them.

If the publisher asks for a 100,000-word science fiction book in one year, then you need to look at what it will take to write it. Chances are you will be excited enough to get the research done in one month. You want to have time to edit the book when you get the first draft done, so you want a couple of months free at the end of writing. This leaves you nine months to write the book. If you take the weekends off, you will have about twenty days a month left to work. This also gives you a few extra days to work if you fall behind. Building leeway into your writing schedule can prevent serious trouble if anything slows you down. Twenty days times nine months will give you a total of 180 days in which to write the actual book. This sounds daunting, doesn't it? However, when you divide 100,000 words by 180 days it comes out to about 556 words per day.

If you cannot write 556 words a day, then you are going to have a difficult time as a professional writer. If being a professional is your goal, then the time to start preparing for it is *before* you get your first contract. Start practising writing five days out of the week. If this is the career you want, then you have to devote the time to it and treat it professionally.

If you are already used to writing 1,000 words a day, you can get your book done well ahead of time or you can take more time off during the writing. Turning the work in early will make you popular with agents and publishers, so it's always something to aim for.

Deciding to write a certain amount a day is only half the equation. The other half is deciding when and where. Some people write better in the mornings, so they find it helpful to get up early and write. Others find they can write well only after the sun is down and everything is quiet, so they take an extra hour at night after everyone has gone to bed. Still others write over their lunch hour at work, or drop by the library on the way home and do a little work. Find your best writing time and make room in your daily schedule to work during that part of the day.

Setting up this sort of schedule for all your novel writing, whether under contract or not, will help prepare you for the day when you are faced with the 'book in a year' problem. This preparation can alleviate a huge amount of pressure for a new author.

Another important aspect of writing is finding the right place to work. Some people have no problem working at the dining room table with kids, television and barking dogs vying for attention. Others need their own corner set up just right, with access to their favourite music. You need to find the place where you are comfortable and not distracted from your imaginary worlds.

So find whatever time and place you are comfortable with. Work on a computer or write by hand. Carve out this bit of time for yourself and stand up for your right to take it. You might try negotiating with the agreement to do something else others in your family may want to do if they give you this time. Until you can show this is a paying job, even those who support your right to write are likely going to have trouble understanding the need to devote yourself to this work. Stick to it, though, because you have a right to pursue your dreams.

What if...

When is your best writing time? Where is the best location? If you have to, look outside the home to libraries and coffee shops for an hour or so of quality writing time. Also be sure you carry either a small paper notebook and pen or a PDA of some sort to take notes at other times.

Writing, rewriting and editing

So, your worldbuilding is done, you've created your characters, and have written an outline to help you move the story along. You have your time and your place for writing – or at least you are trying out various times and locations, to learn what works best for you. Now you are ready to actually write the book – but getting started is turning out to be a problem.

Many people will linger over the background work rather than commit to writing the book itself. They fear that in writing it down, they will fail the vision they've created. This is a common problem because all authors know that nothing they can put down in mere words will ever fully realize what they created in their minds.

This doesn't mean an author should give up and not write the book at all. Obviously, this isn't an answer. Hundreds of other science fiction writers have created works and have drawn readers into their make-believe worlds and held them there with nothing more than words. You can do so as well, as long as you are willing to put in the effort to do the work. This means not only writing, but editing it later as well.

Do not fear writing the book. You cannot ruin it. Your first draft may not be perfect, but that's all right. You can fix it. First drafts are a wonderful gift because they allow you to be daring and to write from the heart without having to worry about perfection. Take advantage of the gift and don't worry about getting the story perfect the first time. There's nothing wrong with correcting glaring errors as you go along, but if you focus too much on making each line right, you risk losing the inspiration that drives the story forward.

Science terms and info dumps

There is one writing problem that especially needs to be addressed for science fiction writers. This is when the author tries to incorporate the science into the story and the work ends up reading like a report instead of a story. Writing information about main sequence stars and which ones are good for human habitation can sound like a lecture in the classroom rather than an exciting passage about exploration.

This often leads to what is commonly known as an 'As you know, Bob' situation: where one character explains something to another one, despite the fact he doesn't need to be lectured about it.

'As you know, Bob, we are looking for a star that falls within the main sequence F, G, and K range, since they are the most likely to support human-like life and have a planet that would be a viable place for us to settle.'

Instead of saying something so blatantly manipulated in order to get the information into the story, try working it into a scene and making it part of the story, like this:

'What's the word?' Bob asked as he came up to the control deck.

Tom looked up from his station and tapped the computer screen. 'We scanned another forty-three F, G and K range stars within two hundred light years, but none of them look suitable or have a planet ready to be settled. That's all right – there are plenty more viable stars out there in the parameters we need. We'll find something.'

When you are dealing with scientific information and terms, it's always good to use the 'show, don't tell' rule of writing. Don't tell the reader what some bit of science means, but rather show how it applies to what they are doing. This is one of the many areas of writing where the author sometimes wants to show all the wonderful information he has collected and correlated in order to make the story scientifically accurate. It is easy to go overboard with such knowledge. Whenever writing up such scenes, it's wise to think about real life and how little we consider the scientific principles by which we live each day. A person rarely considers the complex steps for what it takes to create the electricity when they flick on a switch – at least not until the electricity fails.

Look for interesting places to add information where it isn't going to stand out and where it can be integrated into the storyline so that learning this information will mean more to the reader.

As a writer, you will learn far more about the background then what goes into the actual pages of your novel. The background work is important because it helps you build a unified world and helps you to make logical decisions based on what you know about how things are supposed to work. Knowing the details which make your story work is important, but more important is learning how to use those details wisely so the story doesn't read like a textbook rather than an adventure.

> **What if...**
>
> What if you had a spot in your novel where you needed to introduce information about an alien world, including sea and land masses, gravity and atmosphere. How could you work this into a conversation between two people looking at the world when one of them knows more than the other?

Edit now or later?

Some people edit as they write. If this works for you, that's good – but if, like some, you find you don't finish the work because you get frustrated with the editing, then try writing without stopping to go over every paragraph and page. Those pages will be there later and you may find they are easier to edit after you have the whole of the story before you. It can be quite frustrating to carefully edit material only to find that something later in the story either makes the section superfluous and you end up cutting it, or you significantly change something else which means you have to go back and re-edit this section again to make it fit.

Here is another example of a problem that can arise if you edit while you write and which happens most often with short stories, rather than novels. The author re-reads and edits everything written so far before he starts his work for the day. What happens? The beginning of the story becomes over-edited as he goes over it again and again each day and, while it might be grammatically correct, it lacks style and individuality. The middle section is better because it has been edited but not as much: here, the editing has corrected true mistakes but held on to the power of the original prose style. The ending, however, falls far short because it may only have had a single quick edit after the story was finished.

It is extremely difficult to undo the work when an author over-edits a piece. Authors should always keep copies of their work at various stages (like the first draft, the text after a complete edit, and a finished draft). Sometimes it is possible to go back and recover some aspect of the story that disappeared in edits.

With a novel, and the longer amount of time it takes to write one, the author faces a different problem. A novel can take years to write (if you are not sticking to a schedule and set of goals as suggested above). This means that by the time the author is done with the first draft, chances are that their style has changed and writing ability has improved. The writing and editing in the first part of the book no longer matches the work at the end, and the hard work already done has to be redone anyway. Some writers find this very discouraging and give up the work because they can't stand the idea of facing the editing again.

However, people who write but don't edit as they go face their own problems. The biggest one is that it is far too easy to finish something, set it aside, and never go back to edit it again. They often believe the next story or novel will be better any way, and so why waste the time on editing old material? This leads to writing a great deal, but rarely getting anything ready for submission.

The best solution is to do a little of both writing and editing. Write the story, and do so in the way which is comfortable for you. Don't worry about perfection because no one but you has to see the first draft. Correct mistakes as you see them, but leave major editing until after you are done.

A story or novel is best put aside for a while after the first draft is finished, before the major editing begins. Sometimes, if you are working to a tight schedule, this is not possible. However, if you are able to step away from the work for a few days or weeks, you will have a better chance of finding problems when you do edit. This is because the story will have cleared out of your head, so you will have to read every word and are more likely to notice not only missing words, but areas where the storyline isn't clear or you lack descriptions to make the scene come alive.

Once you are ready to edit, there are several things to keep in mind. Editing can cover various areas from grammar to logical plot progression. Some people cover all these steps in one pass, while others will read first to find story-related problems and afterwards they will go over the material again to make certain of the grammar. You have to be prepared to cut out scenes, characters and entire subplots if they no longer fit as well as you had hoped.

Always save the material, either in a full back-up of an earlier version or in a file made of material you have cut. This is because you may change your mind once you look at the material again.

Make notes of anything you change that you need to carry through to the rest of the manuscript. This includes obvious things like name changes, but it also applies to something like the name of a distant village, the colour of a horse, or the location of a wound. It might prove useful to have either a whiteboard or a corkboard beside your desk where you can keep copies of these notes for easy reference. It can also be helpful to take such notes while actually writing the story, though some people find such breaks intrusive and don't want to take any, especially when the writing is going smoothly.

Having these notes will save you the time of having to look the material up later when you want to remark on the horse or try to remember which leg should have the limp.

Getting outside help

An important part of editing is learning when to let go. If you continue to edit and find that all you are really doing is changing words just to change them, it is time to let go and send the book or story out in submission.

Many people take part in critiquing groups, either live or on the Internet. If so, there are some basic rules which should be applied. First, make certain the story is ready for someone to read, which means making all the corrections you can. Don't waste a critiquer's time on work you can do yourself. Also, always keep track of what you want from the story. If you have others critiquing, chances are they are writers as well – and sometimes it is very hard for a writer to tell the difference between a real problem and just something they would have written differently. A problem often found in face-to-face writing groups is that if the people are not science fiction writers, they may not 'get it'. If so, they may be worse than no help at all as they try to fix things they don't understand. If this turns out to be the case, try presenting them with smaller sections related to their genre, like a romance scene or a section of a mystery. These people can give good critiques, but they may not be able to see the relevant pieces because they freeze at the idea of 'science fiction' and believe they can't help.

Once again, though, don't linger over this work. I've seen people put stories or chapters through critique groups a half dozen times before moving on. At some point there is nothing more to be gained and it becomes an exercise in changing things just to change them.

What if...

Editing is as personal as writing. It can be something authors don't think much about until it becomes a problem. Consider if you would feel comfortable with an online or face-to-face critiquing group. Then think about how you would approach editing your own work.

Two questions to ask about the story

One of the most important things any author should address when writing a novel of any genre, including science fiction, is whether or not the ending meets the expectations created in the rest of the book. For instance, if you started out writing about an impending war with an alien empire, then the war has to be an important part of the book. The war may be diverted in some way (and it had better be an exciting and logical way) but it cannot simply be brushed aside, with the aliens disappearing while the main character goes off on some other adventure.

The writer generally sets out with a question that is posed in the beginning of a novel in some way. The opening scenes create the question and the expectation of an answer. For example, if a shuttle pilot is murdered, then the murder needs to be solved and it has to tie into the rest of the story. There should be no superfluous scenes in a novel. Everything has to tie back to the main plot in some way and all of it has to build up to the ending. The question posed at the start of the book with the murdered shuttle pilot would be a simple one: why?

The other question a science fiction writer needs to ask when looking at the final work is whether or not the science in the story holds up and is sufficiently important to the plot. If you could remove the science fiction elements and still have the same story, then you need to rethink how you can integrate the plot into a science fiction world. There will always be aspects of a story which are timeless and could be transplanted into another genre – love stories, the basics of a mystery, etc. – but there must be something in your book that ties all its elements into a science fiction framework.

So make certain the science remains essential to the story and isn't something added as an afterthought to a scene. Whatever science you use as a basis for your story – hard science, soft science, nanotechnology or anthropology – has to be considered as an intrinsic facet of the story.

Checking the story one last time

Two sections of a book are especially important and need extra care. These are the opening and the ending. If a story does not grab a reader (including an editor or agent) from the start, you cannot expect them to read on further. An opening has to be intriguing and exciting.

An ending has to be memorable and it needs to create a sense of closure for the story. If this book is part of an ongoing series, each novel must still tell a completed story.

In the case of a series (either a trilogy, or stand-alone but related stories), there may be a larger arc with problems needing to be answered, but the single book must have something finished.

In the case of *Broken Journey,* a trilogy might cover three distinct periods in the history of the settlement, starting with Felicia awakening in the first book and ending with her and her companions leaving to start their own settlement away from the others. A second book could cover how the new colony faces survival and deals with the aliens, ending with them overcoming a disaster. The third book could cover reconnecting with the first colony and fighting against aliens intending to destroy them, ending with them overcoming the aliens, written so as to make it obvious that the humans have now found their place and are going to survive.

In other words, each of the three books would have a problem to solve, with the question of their survival always at stake being the overall arc for the complete series. The final book would solve the individual book problem, but it would also answer the question of their own survival, which would be an ongoing theme through all three books.

Make certain your ending is emotionally fulfilling for the reader. This doesn't mean it has to be a happy ending. It does, however, need to be memorable.

> **What if...**
>
> Write a short scene in which someone is heading for work in today's world. Afterwards, write the same scene in a science fiction world set three hundred years in the future. What aspects would be the same? What could you create to make the experience different?

Creating a professional manuscript takes more work than writing the story, but with the proper attitude an author can get through the hard part of editing and preparing the book for the final step.

In the next chapter, we'll look at this final step – preparing a submission package and finding the proper place to send it.

14 This Little Book Went to Market

- Time to move on
- Checking bookshop shelves
- Alternative markets
- Submission packages and query letters
- Synopsis
- Looking professional
- Accepting rejection

In the final chapter of this book, we'll look at what steps the author can take to prepare a manuscript to be sent to a publisher, how to find the right publisher, and how to deal with the inevitable rejections, which are a part of every author's life.

Time to move on

No matter how much you may have enjoyed writing your book, there is a time when you have to move on to the next manuscript. You cannot, however, abandon the work you have done so far.

Every book is a writing and editing experience and will help you grow as an author. Usually, later books will be better than earlier ones – though there are cases where writers get lazy, bored or burnt out and their work suffers for it. You can avoid the first two of these problems by maintaining a good attitude, and the last one by not pushing on when you need a break.

When an author finishes a book, there is often a feeling that it isn't good enough and it would be easier to put it aside and move on. After all, the next one will be better, right? This not just a bad attitude, it can be destructive to the very idea of being a published author. Don't linger, holding on to the book indefinitely. It's far too easy to keep tinkering with a story, or to put it aside with the intention of going over it again later and conveniently forgetting it.

When you start a new story, the previous one might look dull in comparison. This is rarely a valid reaction. New stories always look more interesting because you are dealing with something fresh and unexplored, while you have probably gone over your last manuscript several times already. This can be a problem for writers who allow themselves to be drawn away by new ideas before they finish the first draft of the previous one.

If you have worked through all the previous steps of this book, from worldbuilding through writing and on to editing, then this is not the time to abandon your manuscript. There is one more step you need to take.

It's time to look for a publisher.

Checking bookshop shelves

Where do you send your material? Finding the proper publisher – and their guidelines – is not as hard as it once was. Publishers often have their submission information available on their website. Even if you do not have regular access to a computer with an Internet connection, chances are you can get to one for long enough to find the information you need. A Google search for 'science fiction book publishers' will bring you page after page of information.

Always run a quick background check on any publisher or agent whose name you do not recognize. The Internet is filled with information to help you make a good decision about where to send your material, and conversely about what places to avoid. The Internet, in fact, is one of the best tools invented for writers since the typewriter. There are pitfalls and dangers but, if you approach it carefully and do your research, you can find many publishers for both short and long fiction through online sources.

There are also some books which can help. In the United States, one of the more important is *Writer's Market* from Writer's Digest Publishing and in the UK there is the *Writers' and Artists' Yearbook* from A&C Black Publishers. Both of these books are a wonderful resource for finding publishers.

There is one trick that can help narrow down your search. Check the shelves in bookstores or the pages of magazines to see which ones you like and where you think your work might best fit. For books, if you find there are certain publishers who produce books which you often find appealing then chances are you are writing the same sort of material.

Also, if there is a publisher with covers you dislike, you might want to put them lower on your list for submissions. Authors have no control over the cover art for their work and this might be the only influence you have over the cover you get.

The next step is to find out what you can about the publisher's submission practices, which can usually be done through a search of the Internet. You may find they only take submissions passed to them from agents, in which case you will need to either start approaching agents or else look at other publishers. Since quite a few of the big publishers now take agented submissions only, finding an agent may be a good first step.

Approaching an agent is the same as approaching a publishing market. Agents who sign on authors get a percentage of the sale of books, and they will help direct the author in production of later work. Just as with publishers, make certain you do the work of finding out all you can about the place where you are going to send your work.

An agent can be a helpful person to have on your side. The agent takes care of all submissions and is essential in making certain the author gets the best contract possible. Since many book publishers no longer accept material except through an agent, having one opens up more doors.

Short story authors do not use agents. An agent is paid with a percentage of the payment and payments for short stories are too small to make it worth the work for agents to sell them. This means short story writers generally have it easier for submitting material. They send the story and a cover letter (more on cover letters below). Also they usually don't have to worry about queries and a synopsis, which are typically sent along with book submissions.

> **What if...**
>
> Check out the last ten science fiction books you read and see if there is a single publisher who has put out the majority of them. Take note of it, because chances are the book that you write will be similar to books that you like to read.

Alternative markets

One of the big decisions a writer needs to make when looking at publication is what type of market he or she is interested in pursuing. If your dream has always been to see your book on the shelf at the bookstore, then start with the top publishers who have their places on those shelves. There is no reason to try selling to a small press or electronic publisher first. Start with your dream publication company, but don't be discouraged if it doesn't work out. After working through the top publishers, consider small press and electronic publication.

Avoid any publisher with a bad reputation – those are easy to find via a Google search of their name to see what others are saying about the company. *Never* sign with a publisher who asks you for money because it is a vanity press at best, and a scam at worst. Writers are paid for their work, not the other way around.

If you decide to approach the new world of electronic publishing, look for the same things you would in a print publisher. Make certain the publisher has a good reputation, does not ask for money, and has a traditional submission system where a manuscript must pass through an editor and face the chance of rejection (rather than taking anything offered to them).

Also, be certain to look over the publisher's website and make certain this is a company you want to be associated with. Is your work a good fit with the rest of the material you find there? Is the website itself professional in feel and look? This is the publisher's storefront and people have to be able to easily find work listed there. For book publishers, there should be sample chapters. No one wants to buy a book without seeing if they like how it is written.

Electronic publishing doesn't typically pay as much as the big name print publishers, but some websites may pay as much as you would get from small press print publishers. Several electronic publishers also offer POD (Print on Demand) copies of the work for those who want a paper version of the book.

Print on Demand is a type of technology, like offset printing. It does not indicate the quality of the writing. A few small press companies use POD technology because it allows them to order small runs of books, making it more economical than the offset printing runs. POD technology is also often used for self-publishing.

The last choice open to a writer is to self-publish. I do not suggest writers take this path as their first choice. It is not as easy a road as it looks. While it guarantees the book will be published (either in print or electronically, depending on what the author chooses), it does not guarantee that it will draw readers. Self-publishing requires two very important components: first, the book must be nearly flawless – and unfortunately most writers are blind to their own shortcomings. This is because the author will not have the help of a copy editor to correct the little problems which may have slipped into the manuscript. If you look at self-published books, you will find many of these works are actually not ready to be published and many of the writers have taken this path precisely because they don't want to work harder at editing them.

This ties into the second problem associated with self-publishing. In order to draw readers, the author has to overcome the initial reaction readers have when they learn a book is self-published. Many of them will have looked at the sites promoting self-published books and walked away appalled at the poor quality of material. A good author who chooses to self-publish (and there are a few) has to overcome this bias through an incredible amount of marketing. It is far harder to get sales for a self-published book than for one that comes from a little-known publisher.

All writers must do some marketing of their book. This usually includes having a website of some sort, contacting local media outlets, perhaps doing readings and signings at stores and libraries. If your book is under the imprint of a legitimate publisher, even a small press, this means a professional believed it was good enough to invest money in, to see it produced. This will give the work an automatic first level of acceptance that a self-published book does not have. In fact, self-publishing has a negative start. This may change in the future, however. The Internet has already changed some of the structures of publishing – some companies known for their print publications are now also putting out electronic editions because the market is large enough to warrant the work.

The demographics of the reading public are changing in one odd way. People who have grown up reading on their computer have little trouble with ezines and ebooks and some schools are investing in laptops and electronic textbooks for their students because it is far less expensive than replacing printed books. The more people get used to reading on their computer or handheld device, the more opportunities will develop for both traditional electronic publishing and self-publishing to reach those readers.

There are also niche markets. These are small press or electronic publishers who focus on subgenres and who are often looking for 'edgy' work. They are generally very small with very little distribution capacity. The fans of these markets are usually very picky, but also very dedicated.

Whatever path you decide to take to publication, you always have the opportunity to try something different with the next manuscript you prepare for submission. Choosing one path for a particular work does not mean you are tied to it for everything you write afterwards.

What if...

What do you see the future of publication looking like? If you think print publications are failing, are you ready to make the step in a new direction? Do you think there is room in the market for the diversity of publications already out there, or do you think it is fracturing the readership into too many segments?

Submission packages and query letters

The most important first step in creating a book submission package is to find the publisher's guidelines and stick to them. This is important! The first thing a publisher or agent judges is whether or not the author bothered to check them out before submitting the work. If an editor is going to work with the author for years to come, they need to know that author will act professionally.

A submission package can have several components, depending on what the publisher or agent wants, as set out in their guidelines. A typical submission package will include a cover letter, synopsis and a set number of pages of the actual manuscript. Some publishers may ask for other things, like character descriptions or a novel's timeline.

Some agents and publishers request that the author send them a query first, before sending the full manuscript. The query letter can be somewhat daunting: it is a one page summary of the novel and also includes information such as the author's publication history.

It should be single-spaced with a one inch margin on all sides. The font should be one of the basics: Times New Roman, Courier, or something close to them and at a 12pt size. Do not use fancy fonts, font colours other than black, or fancy paper. If you have a simple masthead paper, use it only if it does not have a professional title on it like lawyer or doctor. Those can be confusing when an editor first glances at the note, and it might get shuffled off to the wrong person by mistake. You can indent paragraphs if you like, but not doing so gives you room to squeeze in a few more words. This can be very important when you are trying to fit so much information into so small an area. You can also make small adjustments to the margins if you find you are only a line or two over the single-page mark, but make certain such adjustments aren't obvious.

The letter can be divided into three main parts, each covering specific information.

Top information

This is where you put your name and address, together with the name and address of the person you are writing to. There is only one very important part of this section and this will require research on your part: do your best to make certain you have the name of the editor or agent. 'Dear Sir or Madam' is not appropriate. Find the name which seems most likely to be the right person and use it. If it turns out the person has left the company or moved to another position, it will still show you made some effort to find the proper person.

If you cannot tell whether the person is male or female, forgo titles like Mr or Ms. Instead use their full name in the salutation: 'Dear Alex Smith' works in a case like this. Put the date between the publisher or agent's address and the salutation. This can be helpful for the person who receives the letter for tracking purposes.

Some people suggest you start the body of the query letter with something like 'I am seeking an agent to represent my book' or a similar line. I think this is unnecessary and obvious, and also it uses up space that is better used for the story summary, since you have very little space as it is.

Middle information: the story summary

The summary of the story is the hardest part of the query letter to write. Think of it as the story told with a very broad brush, ignoring all the subtleties and subplots and hitting only the high points. This includes saying how the story ends. The summary has to sound enticing and interesting. It may take you as long to work out this section of the query letter as it did to write a chapter or two of your novel. It does get easier with practice, though.

Start with the story's opening and introduce the main character and the action and point of the story. Keep it brief. Write a quick idea of what happens in the rest of the book – battles are fought, disaster strikes, etc. – and then close with a short explanation of how the book ends. *Yes, give the ending away.* This isn't a cover blurb meant to entice the reader to buy the book. Agents and editors need to know you have brought the story to a reasonable and satisfying end.

Closing information

In the last section of the query letter, you need to provide some basic information about the book, mention your previous professional publications, and tell them about any reasons why you have special knowledge that helped with the writing of this book. This is another somewhat tricky part.

The first part is easy. In the first sentence, you should give the title of the work, the genre or subgenre, and the approximate word count. Most publishers allow the word processor word count in this case, though some have a special formula you need to use instead. You will find this information in their submission guidelines.

Next is your previous publications information. If you have nothing which can be legitimately added to this section, then skip it. It gives you more room to work with the novel summary again. Every author started out with no previous publications, so it's not a badge of dishonour.

There are certain types of publications you don't want to mention. Don't say you have self-published something unless the work sold thousands of copies. Self-publication tells the publisher nothing important; it cannot tell them that another publisher thought your work professional enough to buy and that's what this little section is about. Some publishers consider self-publication to be a black mark against the author and a sign of a lazy writer.

Also, never mention fanfiction (stories written about television shows, movies, games, etc.) no matter how popular they may have been on a fanfiction website. Fanfiction is, in essence, copyright infringement and some publishers take a very dim view of it.

Do not direct the editor or agent to your website to read material there. Listing your website after your signature is fine, though. If they want to check it out, they will.

Ebook and ezine publications are a grey area for many publishers. You can mention them in passing, or you can go into more detail if there is something by you in this format that has done exceptionally well.

Mostly, though, you want to tell them about your publications in print. This includes small press publications and short story print publications. You don't need to mention them all in great detail. It is enough to let the publisher know they exist.

If you have special knowledge pertaining to the book you are sending them, mention it as well. For *Broken Journey*, a mention of a biology degree (since the main character is a biologist) or classes taken in cultural anthropology as it applies to small village dynamics could be mentioned. If your book is about sailing an alien ocean, then knowledge of sailing craft would be useful. It need not be classroom-related knowledge, as long as it is appropriate to the book.

Do not mention that the book was turned down by someone else. Don't give the editor a negative view of the book by pointing out that someone else said no to it. The only time to mention this is if you were specifically told by another editor or agent to try sending to this place. In that case, mention it in the very first paragraph. This is a referral from a professional publisher, and it will make a good impression. Don't make this part up! Editors and agents talk to each other and the worst thing you can do is lie about receiving a suggestion to send the material on to someone.

Do not mention how your book was critiqued by your writing group. Unless the group has a professionally published member or two who are willing to write cover blurbs for the book, the editor isn't going to care who looked it over for you.

Always include a self-addressed stamped envelope (SASE) with all correspondence, including any subsequent letters you may send, and mention at the bottom of your query letter that you have done so. Some people suggest you send the first five pages of the manuscript, even if it was not listed in the submission instructions. You can do so, but some agents and editors will assume you didn't read the submission guidelines or purposely flouted them, which risks giving a bad impression.

Always check your spelling and grammar. It is easy to overlook something in your query or cover letter when you are excited about sending off your submission. So set the letter aside, at least overnight, and read it again before you do the final printing. Read it aloud, in fact, because sometimes we hear mistakes that we didn't see.

A cover letter can be much the same as a query letter if there has been no previous contact with the publisher or editor. In the case of a short story, the middle summary section can be limited to a general statement about the story with no details since the editor can read the story in one sitting. For novels, the summary section can be shorter if the complete manuscript is included.

In the case of a full manuscript submission, it is wise to add this line at the end, after saying you have included an SASE for their reply: 'The manuscript is disposable'. Back in the dark ages before computers, having the typed manuscript returned to you was very important. Now it's easier and cheaper to print out a new, pristine copy to send to the next publisher on your list. If for some reason you do want the manuscript back, be certain you include enough postage on the SASE for its return.

The most important part in all this is to follow the publisher's guidelines and to recheck the spelling and grammar on everything you are going to send them. These sheets of paper are representing you to a future employer for a job you really want. So make certain the submission package gives a good impression.

What if...

It can be helpful to practise writing query letters before you are ready to submit anything. For this exercise, you can write one using an unfinished manuscript or an older manuscript. You can even try practising this by writing one based on someone else's published novel. The hardest part to write is the middle section, so practise this by writing short descriptions of various works.

Synopsis

A synopsis is nothing more than an outline in paragraph format. It can be long or short (check the guidelines to see if the publisher or agent has a preference) and is usually very easy to write. In fact, if a publisher asks for an outline of a story, it usually means he wants a synopsis. This can cause some confusion, though, and it might be a good idea to ask what the publisher actually wants.

A simple way to generate a synopsis is to write one or two descriptive paragraphs about every chapter in your book and then edit those paragraphs to make them coherent and exciting. The synopsis should have the same general feel as the book. In other words, if you have written a comedic story make certain the comedy comes through in the synopsis.

This is not a dry recitation of the facts. The story has to sound compelling and exciting. It has to show you have an interesting opening section, a strong middle, and a compelling and logical ending.

The synopsis is told in present tense and third person format. When the story is told in first person (*I awoke to look into the face of a stranger*) the synopsis version is translated into third person (*Felicia awakes to look into the face of a stranger*). However, since you don't want to surprise the editor or agent later, it is wise to tell them about the style of the book. In this case the opening line to the synopsis might be written like this:

> *Felicia (First Person POV character) awakes to look into the face of a stranger.*

Don't try to race through the synopsis, though. Do your best to make it interesting. Think of it as talking about your story to a friend: you are not going to hit every single point in the story when you discuss it, but you will cover all the high points.

It might help to divide the synopsis into three sections, just like in writing the book itself. Devote equal space to the beginning, middle and ending. If the publisher asks for a short synopsis (which can sometimes be as little as one or two pages) stick to the main storyline. If the publisher wants a longer synopsis, cover some of what goes on in subplots as well.

If you have an outline for the book this can also help you to generate a synopsis, though be careful if you have changed some of the material as you wrote. Sometimes, though, looking at the original outline can help to clarify the story's progress and make it easier to describe the storyline without getting bogged down in the details, despite how much you may love them – and you should love them, of course!

Keep the synopsis as exciting and fast-moving as you can manage. Include not only the action, but also some of the characters' motivations and emotional reactions.

Looking professional

Sending a manuscript off to a publisher or agent can be frightening. We want perfection and acceptance, but most manuscripts will never see professional publication and sometimes it has nothing to do with the quality of the work. There are a limited number of places available to be filled. To win one of those coveted spots, you have to act professionally when you submit stories, you have to present a unique vision, and you have to be lucky. Yes, luck does come into it.

The easy part is to send off professional-looking material and this will put you far ahead of most submissions. Many people don't bother to read submission guidelines, learn proper grammar, spell-check their material, or do any of the other easy things that help make the submission stand out from the crowd. Those people who do not take the time to make their submission look professional will find their work will be consistently rejected.

Some of the basics of query and cover letter formatting apply to full story submissions as well. Use plain white paper and black ink, and always use one of the basic fonts like Times New Roman or Courier. Most publishers ask for one inch margins on all sides, double spacing, and left hand justified formatting (that is, with the manuscript page having a ragged right side).

There may be special instructions, so – as always – read the guidelines before you submit. If you are uncertain about something, you can email or call the publisher to ask, or do your best to follow the instructions. As long as you have followed the basics points set out above as best you can, you will still be far ahead of most people.

Accepting rejection

A publisher or agent typically receives large numbers of submissions, sometimes numbering the hundreds, each week. The first task of an editor or agent when they look at the submission pile isn't to find something good, but rather to quickly reject anything which can be passed over without too much work. When the pile is then reduced down to a manageable size, their work turns to the story itself. But first they will look for the easy ones to put aside: this means submissions from people who plainly don't have a clue what they are doing, have ignored the submission guidelines, sent the wrong genre, etc.

After the first group has been rejected – which will be the majority of submissions – then the editor or agent will begin judging the rest of the material on the basis of whether or not the story suits their market.

Your story may not make it through, but if you are careful with the technical side of writing then you will have a far better chance of selling than many people will ever have – because they think to write something and send it off is enough. Chances are you will have many rejections before you have a sale. This is a normal part of the author's world and the only ones who succeed in this business are the ones who do not give up.

Once you send a submission off to the publisher, move on. Start your next project, because no writer can make a career on one sale. Submissions often take a long time before you receive an answer and even then it is likely to be a rejection. So it will help to have another project already moving forward.

If you get a rejection, look over your material again to make certain there is nothing you want to change and then send it off once more. Keep doing so until you have tried every viable market. If you get to the end of your list and still haven't sold the story, consider the alternative publishers (if you haven't already).

Letting go of a work and sending it off to the publisher is one of the most difficult, and often frightening, aspects of being a writer. Some people so fear the idea of their work being rejected that they never send out anything at all.

The truth is that no one is ever rejected. A story might be turned down, but this is not personally directed at the author.

Sometimes a story will be turned down for reasons you simply cannot guess ahead of time. The editor may have a pet dislike of red-haired women like your main character, or he may have recently bought something very similar to your story. The editor might have had a headache and hated everything he read on the day he received your submission.

If you are very lucky, you will get a personal rejection slip with a few notes rather than a form rejection. Sometimes a personal rejection slip is a sign of having drawn the editor's attention. However, if you do not get one, this does not mean the story was horrible. The editor may have been too busy to write something or the editor might not give personal rejections at all.

Never take rejections personally. If you get a rejection with some advice, look it over and decide if the advice suits what you are trying to do with the story. Sometimes an editor might miss a point in the story or might put his own ideas in when he reads it. Always weigh any suggestions against what you want to write. It is your story. You get the final say.

What if...

One of the things people like to do is to keep a collection of their rejection slips. These are badges of honour in the world of writing and show that the person is serious about publication. Why not prepare a notebook or special box for rejections now, so that you are ready for them?

Epilogue
Finding your own path

This book has covered subjects ranging from creating aliens to building colonies on other worlds, and from character creation to preparing a manuscript for publishers. However, a book of this sort can't teach you how to be a good science fiction writer. It can only be a guide to help you consider the myriad possibilities open to you. Every science fiction writer has to head into new territory and find their own path to something wondrous. This is the most essential part of writing science fiction: you must be willing to step beyond today's reality and imagine something all your own.

When it comes to writing, figure out what works for you. When reading books like this, you may find bits and pieces of things which help you, but you will combine those into something distinctively your own. We are all unique in our talents and our needs and, though we can point out paths to others, those people will wander off in their own directions.

Be willing to look in different places for the knowledge you have not yet found – the little nudge that clarifies a missing link between your mind and the words on the screen or paper on which you work.

A science fiction writer, more than any other type of fiction writer, has to be open to learning new things. If you spend time reading non-fiction books on various subjects, it will help build depth into your books. Don't settle for only reading books about the sciences, either. There is a great deal to learn from history, economics, philosophy – and sometimes from books about writing. So explore what your world has to offer and use that knowledge to build an entire new world from what you learn.

Be ready to go out and explore everything, because science fiction is all about exploration of places no one but you can see. No one else can imagine what you imagine. If a group of writers were all handed exactly the same story idea, they would not write the same book. Your work is unique: that uniqueness is its greatest quality.

So when people ask you (again) why you write science fiction instead of something 'real' remember you have the greater imagination to see beyond the narrow walls of reality.

Robert Heinlein said that everything is theoretically impossible, until it is done. This is an excellent view of science fiction. What you write may not always be theoretically possible today, but never rule out what humanity will learn to do tomorrow.

Isaac Asimov's words on science fiction are perhaps the most profound:

> *Individual science fiction stories may seem as trivial as ever to the blinder critics and philosophers of today – but the core of science fiction, its essence has become crucial to our salvation if we are to be saved at all.*

Those of us who write science fiction are the dreamers who will help to make tomorrow's worlds. Don't be afraid to imagine what they will be like. Go and explore your paths and write the stories only you can bring to the world. We need those dreams of the future.

Reading List for Science Fiction

You cannot understand the depth of possibilities in science fiction without reading a variety of the works available. If you are going to write science fiction, then you must read it as well.

While great newly-published science fiction books hit the shelves every year, some authors and books have withstood the test of time. Science fiction, by its very nature, often resists becoming dated, though admittedly some do fall by the wayside. While the *John Carter of Mars* books by Edgar Rice Burroughs could be, at best, accepted as an alternate universe science fiction today, they are still fun to read.

Below is a list of authors with short discussions of some of their works. There are many other wonderful authors and great books in the science fiction genre, so this is only a small sampling. Some of the books listed here are true classics and others are relatively new but have created milestones in the genre.

Not all science fiction books will appeal to even the most ardent science fiction fan. However, a science fiction writer should sample as much as possible. You cannot grok something until you have come to understand it. And if you do not know the origin of the word 'grok' you have not read at least one important classic in science fiction!

Douglas Adams

Science fiction is not well known for having a sense of humour, but the late Douglas Adams broke out of the serious mould with such wonderful books as *Hitchhiker's Guide to the Galaxy*, *So Long and Thanks for all the Fish*, and *Dirk Gently's Holistic Detective Agency*. Gifted with a talent for making fun of science fiction tropes, he won over many readers in a genre that often takes itself far too seriously.

Isaac Asimov

Asimov was an incredibly prolific author who wrote both science fiction and science fact, with a total of over 500 books he either wrote or edited. He had an incredible ability to weave stories out of science in ways that have drawn in readers for decades. One of his most famous works is *The Foundation Series*, which he wrote over a 44-year time period. In it, he created a type of mathematics used to predict the future but only on a large scale. His robot stories, which include novels and shorter work, set out the three laws of robotics and have been credited with influencing the creation of the character Lt. Commander Data from the *Star Trek: the Next Generation* television series.

Ray Bradbury

In April of 2007, Ray Bradbury was awarded a Pulitzer Prize in recognition of his influential career. With works like *Fahrenheit 451* and *The Martian Chronicles*, he was one of the first science fiction writers to reach across genre lines and pull in readers who normally would not have looked at such books. He is prolific and continues to please his readers with new offerings.

John Brunner

With *Stand on Zanzibar*, John Brunner brought the subgenre of sociological science fiction to life, winning both the Hugo award and the British Science Fiction Award in 1969. That story, about the problems of over-population, also looked at trends in technology and the philosophy of eugenics. His novel *Shockwave Rider* is considered a pre-cyberpunk book that deals with a software program that replicates itself across a computer network.

C. J. Cherryh

C. J. Cherryh's outstanding career is filled with incredibly well-written and exciting science fiction tales. *Downbelow Station* and *Cyteen*, both Hugo award winners, are books set in her Alliance-Union universe. The *Foreigner Sequence* books are an intriguing look at human and alien relationships on a world where the two groups are living in forced seclusion from one another in order to keep human technology from overpowering the alien society. Filled with adventure and fascinating looks at an alien culture, it's a series of books that should be on the shelf of every science fiction reader.

Arthur C. Clarke

Best known for *2001: A Space Odyssey*, Arthur C. Clarke provided readers with exciting novels for over fifty years until his death in 2008. *Childhood's End*, a story about the next step in human evolution and contact with aliens, is often considered one of his best works. Much like Asimov, he had a flair for writing non-fiction as well, and his prescient essays on the use of geostationary satellites as telecommunications links have had a more profound effect on our world than the work of any other science fiction writer. Clarke's excellent, clean writing style means his books continue to be favourites decades after they were written.

Samuel R. Delaney

Chip Delaney is one of the most eloquent and daring writers in the world of science fiction. With novels like *Babel 17* and *Dhalgren*, and shorter works such as *Time Considered as a Helix of Semi-Precious Stones*, this writer has carved out a unique place in the genre. His astounding ability with language and his unusual range of characters and story situations moves him outside the usual range of science fiction authors.

Philip K. Dick

People often know a number of Philip K. Dick's works, even if they have never read one of his books: the movies *Blade Runner*, *Total Recall* and *Minority Report* were each based on his written material, as were several other lesser known movies and shows. His explorations of metaphysical and political themes draw fans back time and again. Besides his well-known story *Do Androids Dream of Electric Sheep?* (the basis for *Blade Runner*), works like *The Man in the High Castle* have set the standard for alternate history books.

Gordon R. Dickson

With the *Dorsai* books, Gordon R. Dickson gave us a great series of tales based around a military group. The *Dorsai* books are examples of a subgenre, military science fiction, that has grown over the years but his contribution has seldom been bettered. Dickson had a wonderful feel for the world of the mercenaries he created. With *Tactics of Mistake*, he paved the way for much of the popular military science fiction that followed.

Robert Heinlein

Many of Robert Heinlein's early works are now classified as young adult books, although they remain popular with adult readers. However, it was with *Stranger in a Strange Land* that Heinlein helped the science fiction genre to 'grow up'. It is the story of Valentine Michael Smith, the only survivor of a failed settlement on Mars, and his return to Earth after being raised by the Martians. The book deals with the questions of what it means to be human, as well as religious beliefs and how easy it is for humans to turn on each other. There are two versions of this book available. The older one is the original release (by far the better of the two). The second is the unedited version – which proves that even the greatest authors needed a little editing along the way. This book uses the term 'grok', which essentially means to understand something so completely you become a part of it.

Frank Herbert

Although Frank Herbert wrote a number of science fiction tales, it is *Dune* for which he is best known. This novel escaped the mould of traditional science fiction and gave readers a fantastic world filled with mystical powers and prophecy. The world of *Dune* is a dangerous place filled with rebel freemen and assassins, but it is also the world that holds the key to controlling the empire. *Dune* transcends the science fiction genre with its almost fantasy-like feel, yet it delivers a science fiction tale which continues to fascinate readers.

Ursula K. Le Guin

Part of the Hanish series of stories, *The Left Hand of Darkness* is considered one of the earliest and best representatives of feminist science fiction. On the world of Gethen the people are neuter for all but two days out of the month, at which time they can be either male or female, based on who is their partner. A representative of the Ekumen has come to draw the world into the federation of worlds but finds himself caught in a web of political intrigue. A major theme in the novel is obviously one of gender roles, and around this topic Le Guin has woven an exciting story which continues to intrigue readers and leave them asking their own questions about such roles.

Larry Niven and Jerry Pournelle

These two writers prove that a solid science background and imagination work well together. As individual authors and in collaboration, they wrote some of the best science fiction produced from the 1970s to the 2000s. Larry Niven's *Known Universe* books, along with the collection of stories he wrote with Jerry Pournelle, are staples of the science fiction world. *Ringworld*, one of the many great tales in this collection, is an exciting adventure set in a hard science story filled with great characters and spectacular scenery. With Jerry Pournelle, Niven wrote *The Mote in God's Eye*, which introduces us to an extraordinary alien civilization, also *Lucifer's Hammer*, the tale of a meteorite strike and the fall of civilization.

Jerry Pournelle has also written several science fiction books of his own, including *King David's Spaceship* and his well known *Janissaries* series. Combining his talents with Larry Niven has helped create some exceptional tales.

Andre Norton

When she began publishing science fiction and fantasy books in 1934, the genre was still a 'man's world' and Alice Mary Norton wrote under a male pseudonym. In some ways, her early years mirrored those of Robert Heinlein while he was still writing young adult material. Although Heinlein moved onto the 'adult' realm, Norton remained true to her origins and continued to produce exciting adventure stories into the 1990s. Her 'Forerunners', aliens long gone from the scene when the humans arrived, presented a unified story universe as they turned up in her books. The *Solar Queen* stories, *Time Traders* stories, and many others continued to delight loyal readers for decades.

Kim Stanley Robinson

The *Mars Trilogy* (*Red Mars, Green Mars, Blue Mars*) is filled with enough science to entertain the hard science fiction reader, along with enough fascinating characters to hold the attention of people who prefer softer science fiction. This chronicle of settlement on Mars is a fascinating story weaving science, politics and human ingenuity into the story of a planet transformed. Epic in vision and incredibly detailed, this book managed to make even the world of Mars seem like another character in the story.

Selected Bibliography

Books

Bova, Ben (1987) *Welcome to Moonbase*. New York: Ballantine Books.

Bronowski, J. (1973) *The Ascent of Man*. London, BBC.

Considine, Douglas M. (Editor) (1976) *Van Nostrand's Scientific Encyclopedia*. New York: Van Nostrand Reinhold Company.

Harman, William K. (2003) *A Traveler's Guide to Mars*. New York: Workman Publishing.

Hawking, Stephen (1988) *A Brief History of Time*. London: Bantam Books.

Levy, David H. (Editor) (2000) *The Scientific American Book of the Cosmos*. New York: St. Martin's Press.

Ludlum, David M. (1991) *The Audubon Society Field Guide to North American Weather*. New York: Alfred A. Knopf.

Narita, George M. (Editor) (1975) *Grzimek's Animal Life Encyclopedia, Volume 11*. New York: Van Nostrand Reinhold Company.

Ochoa, George and Jeffrey Osier (1993) *Writer's Guide to Creating a Science Fiction Universe*. Cincinnati, Ohio: Writer's Digest Books.

Pinker, Steven (1994) *The Language Instinct*. New York: Harper Perennial.

Ridley, Matt (1999) *Genome*. New York: Harper Perennial.

Audio

Titchener, Frances (2004) *To Rule Mankind and Make the World Obey*, Barnes and Noble, Portable Professor.

Websites

Animal Diversity Web, http://animaldiversity.ummz.umich.edu/site/index.html

Atmospheric Sciences, http://www.atmos.uiuc.edu/index.html

Australian Telescope Outreach and Education, http://outreach.atnf.csiro.au/

Library Thing, http://www.librarything.com

Ralan's SpecFic and Humor Webstravaganza, http://www.ralan.com

The Atmosphere, http://teachertech.rice.edu/Participants/louviere/atmos.html

Wikipedia, http://www.wikipedia.org/

Index

Adams, Douglas 209
Aliens 2, 7, 13, 16, 28, 34, 35, 38, 39, 55, 87, 95, 98, 115, 120, 124, 125, 144, 147, 150, 151, 153, 154, 157, 161, 162, 182, 183, 201, 205, 208
  building construction 71–2
  characters 62, 63, 69, 72, 138–40
  creation 57–66
  communications 116–18
  culture 67–74, 155–6
  language 75, 77–81
  names 73–4
  technology 67–74, 155–6
Alternate history 16, 123, 205
Androids 40, 43, 44, 121, 143, 205
Anthropology 8, 12, 27, 182, 194
Artificial Intelligence (AI) 31, 40, 44, 133
Asimov, Isaac 9, 11, 43, 202, 204, 205
Atmosphere 30, 48, 95, 178, 210
  clouds 53, 54
  creature creation 58–61
  ionosphere 52
  mesosphere 52
  orographic lifting 54
  stratosphere 52
  thermosphere 52
  troposphere 52
  worldbuilding 52–5

Behaviour 61, 65, 66, 71, 72, 74
Biomes 45, 55
  understanding of 49–51

Black holes 46, 98
Bradbury, Ray 15, 204
Brunner, John 15, 93, 204
Buildings 39, 49, 57, 64, 80, 85
  alien constructions 71–2
Bussard Ramjet 97

Cell Phones 4
Character 4, 5, 10, 12, 14, 15, 18, 28, 48, 55, 78, 80, 81, 85, 86, 87, 89, 90, 101, 103, 108, 115, 121, 122, 123, 125, 126, 176, 177, 180, 182, 191, 192, 194, 196, 197, 199, 201, 204, 205, 207, 208
  alien characters 62, 63, 69, 72, 73–4, 138–40
  character and story 147–71
  character creation 21, 22, 24
  characters and space travel 93–6
  creating characters 127–45
  worldbuilding and characters 30, 31, 35, 36, 39, 42
Clarke, Arthur C. 4, 5, 44, 205
Clones 32, 40, 41–2, 121
Clothing 81, 84, 117
  clothing and worldbuilding 64–6
Clouds 53, 54
Colonies 16, 23, 33, 36, 83, 86, 88–90, 102, 104, 113, 116, 117, 118, 143, 144, 201
  colonies and Religion 38–9

211

government   113, 116–18
outside of Earth   88–90
Computers   4, 15, 40, 44, 59, 67, 71, 161, 195
Cultural anthropology   8, 27, 194
Culture   15, 23, 27, 29, 34, 35, 36, 38, 40, 44, 55, 57, 63, 74, 77, 80, 84, 101, 102, 114, 115, 117, 118, 136, 138, 144, 147, 159, 164, 205
future culture   151–5
technology, form and culture   67–72
Cyberpunk   8, 14, 15, 16, 107, 204
Cyborgs   40, 42, 43

Delany, Samuel R.   17
Dick, Philip K.   15, 16, 43, 121, 205
Dickson, Gordon R.   17, 206
Domes   26, 33, 36, 37, 45, 46, 88, 89, 90, 96, 114, 118
Dystopian   1, 15

Einstein   41, 102, 123

Fantasy   4, 5, 18, 20, 98, 122, 160, 206, 207
Faster-than-light travel   4, 9, 13, 98, 121
Fission   97, 98
Fusion   46, 98

Gibson, Walter   15, 16
Government   15, 16, 24, 104, 105, , 131, 157, 163
types of   107–18
Gravity   44, 46, 48, 49, 52, 55, 59, 60, 61, 63, 67, 87, 88, 95, 96, 123, 151, 156, 178

Habitat   50, 58, 63, 64, 88
Habitation   49, 176
Hard science fiction   7, 8, 9, 10, 11, 13, 16, 95, 208
Heinlein, Robert   16, 17, 18, 41, 44, 99, 122, 202, 206, 207, 208

History   13, 16, 21, 33, 34, 71, 84, 87, 118, 122, 123, 144, 183, 191, 201, 205, 209
history and religion   37–40

Internet   4, 10, 22, 24, 46, 76, 88, 120, 121, 180, 186, 187, 190
Ionosphere   52

Liaden universe   18
Language   20, 71, 73, 74, 84, 138, 153, 205, 209
language in the future   75–81
Lee, Sharon   18
Legends   63
Le Guin, Ursula   17, 207

Magnitude   102
Mass   41, 46, 47, 48, 97, 98
Mesosphere   52
Military science fiction   17, 206
Miller, Steve   18
Moon   2, 44, 45, 48, 85, 94, 152
colonies on the moon   86–9
Moon, Elizabeth   17
Mutations   40, 41
Myth   39, 40, 63, 66, 140, 160

Nanotechnology   8, 10, 30, 31, 99, 182
Niven, Larry   10, 11, 16, 17, 40, 94, 98, 207
Norton, Andre   16, 18, 207, 208
Nuclear   5, 17, 33, 34, 97

Orographic lifting   54
Orwell, George   15
Outlines, traditional   160, 167

Population   14, 35, 38, 41, 42, 48, 90, 114, 154, 204
Post-apocalyptic   5, 8, 14, 17, 23, 30, 94, 129
Psychic   4, 13

Religions   38, 39
Robots   40, 43, 126, 143

Satellites   4, 85, 86, 87, 116, 152, 205
Self-publishing   189, 190, 193
Sense of wonder   7
Soft science fiction   7, 8, 9, 12, 13, 16, 20
Space station   46, 49, 88, 96
Speculative fiction   7, 20
Stars   17, 18, 45, 46, 47, 48, 79, 95, 96, 97, 98, 116, 158, 176, 177
Steele, Allen   100, 104
Stratosphere   52

Taboos   38, 63
Thermosphere   52

Time travel   9, 13, 119, 120, 122, 123, 124
Troposphere   52

Verne, Jules   2, 5
Virtual reality   30, 31

Warfare   33, 34
Weather   26, 30, 32, 45, 59, 95, 151, 209
weather and worldbuilding   50–5
Wells, H. G.   9, 16, 122
Worldbuilding   21, 22, 28, 29, 30, 35, 39, 44, 45, 49, 57, 63, 68, 77, 83, 85, 89, 94, 95, 123, 127, 129, 137, 138, 140, 143, 147, 176, 186
Wow factor   7